# Rewire Your Brain

*Change Your Mind and Habits for a Better Life Without Anxiety. Neuroscience and EFT Tapping + 100 Positive Affirmations to Increase Productivity, Wealth, Health and Weight Loss*

John Hanson

The content and information contained in this book has been compiled from sources deemed reliable, and it is accurate to the best of the Author's knowledge, information and belief. However, the Author cannot guarantee its accuracy and validity and cannot be held liable for any errors and/or omissions. Further, changes are periodically made to this book as and when needed. Where appropriate and/or necessary, you must consult a professional (including but not limited to your doctor, attorney, financial advisor or such other professional advisor) before using any of the suggested remedies, techniques, or information in this book.

Upon using the contents and information contained in this book, you agree to hold harmless the Author from and against any damages, costs, and expenses, including any legal fees potentially resulting from the application of any of the information provided by this book. This disclaimer applies to any loss, damages or injury caused by the use and application, whether directly or indirectly, of any advice or information presented, whether for breach of contract, tort, negligence, personal injury, criminal intent, or under any other cause of action.

You agree to accept all risks of using the information presented inside this book.

You agree that by continuing to read this book, where appropriate and/or necessary, you shall consult a professional (including but not limited to your doctor, attorney, or financial advisor or such other advisor as needed) before using any of the suggested remedies, techniques, or information in this book.

# Table of Contents

# Description

I saw people around me messing with life and dealing with stress and anxiety. The writing in this book is based on my observations of people's life and some personal experience of dealing and fighting with anxiety. It is natural to become anxious at some point in life. I too dealt with anxiety when I had certain failures in my career. I decided to take up some positive motivations by reading some books. I talked to my friends and family about my stress; they give me encouragement to come out of my situation by advising some positive affirmations. I started writing this book when I realized that my dark time where I was depressed just became a past from which I have moved on by asserting positive thoughts and some and exercises to release anxiety. I want to share my experience of life in the form of affirmations which really helped me to release all my negativity towards life and made me a positive person.

Affirmations are the encouragement which when practiced everyday can change our way of life. This book contains 100 positive affirmations which can be practiced by common man in in their daily life without putting much effort towards it. Our thoughts are very powerful in controlling our life This book draws your attention towards the different things in life which can be managed by our thoughts.

This book is written in in layman language making it convenient for everyone to read.As I started writing more ideas popped into my mind. To make this book present table a lot of typing Re typing thinking modifications has been done. This book also put some light on recent researches published done by University and published in papers Be a science student and a voracious reader I I gained knowledge in neuroscience and Technology by reading articles on recent researches. und out many recent researches done by Neurologist and psychologist on rewiring of brain. I want to share some of my knowledge on this.

Some of our major activities like ok sleep eating habits and exercise not only affects our Physical health what also affects our mental health. By keeping this activity in proper balance, you can have a proper balance in your life.I have mentioned about the different ways to release anxiety like practicing mindfulness exercise, physical exercise, meditation, EFT tapping and hundred positive affirmations

After on the evaluations of given Idea and wisdom it depends upon the reader to accept it to his life levels. For the benefits of my reader I suggest them to read this book with an open heart to accept all the affirmations and to reshape their mind to lead a positive life and release and anxiety. I have put all my efforts and thoughts to make this book affect your soul. Enjoy reading all the topics and affirmations which has some examples related to you real life.I hope after reading this book my readers will drain down all their negative emotions and Desire and fill their heart and mind with love and positiveness.

# Introduction

A person is exposed to new stimulus every day which his mind captures and saves. He gets new information and remembers it for a certain period of time as long as it is important for him. Though it safe that information, it needs to be recalled every once in a while to be remembered. When the phrase 'rewiring your brain' comes, neuroplasticity is the scientific term for it, with which means remolding our brain to learn new experiences feelings,  emotions and data. The neuroplastic experiment was first done by Russian psychologist Ivan Pavlov in 1899.

He gave the theory of classical conditioning while he was studying the digestive system of dogs. In his laboratory he kept a dog in controlled condition without providing food. When food was provided to the dog, it salivated and Pavlov measured the amount of saliva secreted by the dog. Pavlov concluded that the salivating action of dog was a natural stimulus.

The next time, he rang the bell prior to giving the dog food, the dog was able to hear the bell before seeing the food and then it started to salivate. Pavlov continued this experiment for some days and a condition came when the dog started to salivate only on the hearing of the bell even though food was not given. Pavlov took this sample of saliva and measured it and found out that it was of the same quantity as before when the dog salivated with natural stimulus on presentation of food. On this, he concluded that if two things which are unrelated and presented together for a period of time then we learn to relate these two things with each other in the same way as the dog-related ring of bell with food.

This is conditioned learning in which mind Learns a reflex and responses to it without thinking too much about it. In the following chapters you are going to learn about the recent researches done by University of Barcelona, University of Rochester and Carnegie Mellon University on neuroplasticity. The chapters also contain journals published recently in Science and Technology and human welfare and a current paper published in journal addiction biology. In our day-to-day life we come across a lot of things which stresses our mind makes us anxious and distressed. We generally take these hurdles of life too seriously and lose our calm. The following chapters explain how our brain words and react two different kinds of anxieties and its therapy. It will provide you with affirmations that will help you to release your nervousness towards everything and make you a

more well-built person.

# Chapter 1: New research on neuroplasticity according to psychology and neuroscience

*Figure 1: Free Credits*

According to recent research, neuroscientists suggest that social inequalities can permanently affect our brains. Those who are affected by this inequality are neurobiological poor. According to a journal published recently in Science and Technology and human values, it has also become common for researchers to use this idea to reframe social issues like poverty in neurological terms. This paper is on the regarding of the issue that how these social issues reframe our neurological system. Feminism, religious issues, gender issues, country issues, freedom issues, and government issues, has framed our minds to think ok in a new way.

Study conducted by the University of Barcelona,2019 has it that. This paper is in the reference that if in any case the left brain gets damaged during early childhood the right brain can take over its function. Young brains are more plastic then old brains, they can easily reorganize themselves and do all functions a child's brain can reshape itself wire neuroplasticity In response to trauma. If an adult suffers from any kind of brain damage then and it's hard for him to recover. But in case of phone your old young child his other hemisphere of the brain can easily take up the function of the damaged part.

A device called Portable Neuromodulation Stimulator (PoNs), is found just on the surface of the tongue and delivers high-frequency to mild electrical impulses as the patient goes through an intense routine of daily physiotherapy. This device is a part of intense workout like an hour working on a treadmill. It can help people to increase their mobility and balance and can cure visual impairment.

Research done by a professor at the University of Rochester and Carnegie Mellon University explained that even after a stroke the eye and brain connections remain intact and if these connections are well understood it can be cured by therapies which enhance neuroplasticity with the intention of restoring the ability to see in patients. This study focuses on patients who have survived stroke and how best they can recover their vision. 15 patients underwent an MRI in a bid to find out areas of brain and evaluate the integrity of cells in retina. Research showed that though some cells maintained health, the patient could not see and respond in the process of seeing. Selective Serotonin Reuptake Inhibitor, the antidepressant Prozac which are attributed to enhancing neuroplasticity to rescind functions after damage was the drug used. The drug forms new connections between areas of the brain necessary for interpreting signals from the healthy sight.

The vanishing effect of Nicotine on the brain of rats by motor-skill training has been described in a current paper published in the Journal Addiction Biology. A specific pattern of changes occurred in the brain of rats associated with motivation, habit formation and finally reward. A group of rats was provided with nicotine for 3 weeks, which is enough for them to create a lifelong effect. After the three weeks of nicotine mouse were trained to balance on a rotating rod called rotarod. A controlled group of rats was not trained to balance on rotarod. The control group of mice showed decreased condition of neural activities and the trained group of mice showed increased neural activity. Researchers concluded that after leaving nicotine if the mind is exposed to new motor reflexes it forms new neural connections by neuroplasticity.

**Anxiety**

Anxiety is a disorder of taking too much tension about your work, life, relationships, future, and your past. It's a phobia of failure of doing your daily chores. Our mind becomes fixed in getting worried about a thing rather than concentrating on all other important things. a little anxiety is good but filling your mind with a lot of and anxiousness can irritate you, make you distressful and cause illness.

Different kind of mental energies comes from doing different work. We should keep a balance of all energies within us. Keeping some amount of stress is also good because it makes us more responsible for our life and keeping positive energies encourages us to complete that task. Without keeping a balance between good and bad energies we cannot fulfill our purpose in life. Like everything is balanced between advantages and disadvantages likes and dislikes and success and failure we need to keep a balance of everything in our life starting from us our preferences and our decisions to our family friends relationship and job.

Some symptoms of anxiety are-

- Feeling restless

- Finding difficult to concentrate
- Nausea
- High blood pressure
- Sweating even in cold temperature
- High heart rate
- Feeling exhausted
- Thinking of giving up
- Realizing of mistakes

## Thoughts of social scientists on anxiety

Anxiety can be because of many causes, it may be of starting something new, like if you join a new office you might be nervous of new colleagues, new boss and new environment and find it difficult to adjust there but as time passes you become more comfortable and friendly with your environment and the anxiety of nervousness vanishes off but for some people the anxiety level is so high that it remains for a longer period of time which affects their work efficiency. They always feel nervous to talk to their colleagues and boss about work; they feel insecure in their environment. This could affect their work because their concentration is only upon being anxious and uncomfortable in their surroundings.

Being anxious around family and feeling comfortable in between your friends can affect your relationship with others. The feeling of anxiousness may last for more than 6 months. This kind of anxiousness where you feel uncomfortable around everybody and find it hard to talk to anybody is called social anxiety disorder. Here people fear being judged negatively, therefore they cannot progress in public speaking getting close to friends and colleagues.

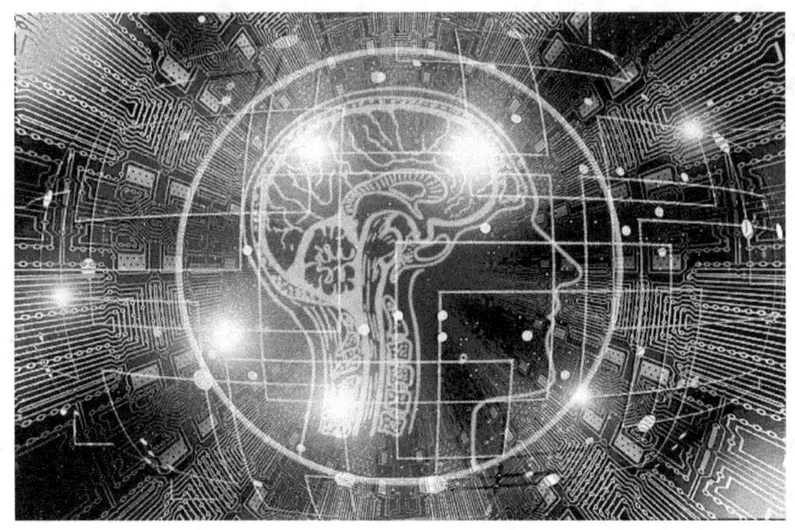

*Figure 2: Free Credits*

## Thoughts of neuroscience on anxiety

Stress and anxiety are a good physical response to be serious about our work it helps in keeping us sharp and active towards our work. Short-term stress improves alertness, memory, and motivation. But stress should not be too high that rather than motivating us it demotivates us.

Generalized Anxiety Disorder' is persistent, exclusive and unrealistic worry about everyday things. Anxiety disorder has grown a lot of fame in the United States having every five adults with this trait. This is the result of research carried out by Anxiety and depression Association of America and the National Mental Health Institute.

As the different parts of brain functions for different senses and emotions for example the temporal lobe processes sound and the occipital lobe processes vision, there are different regions for different emotions in our brain.

There is a limbic system in our brain which is a complex part consisting of the thalamus, hypothalamus, amygdala and hippocampus. This circuit is believed to be responsible for most of our emotions. The prefrontal cortex is keen to integrating these signals for decision making.

## Why our bad habits die so hard

When you are aware of the resulting factors to your ill behavior, you are in a better position to counter them. Habits come and go in a bid to take over the body. This is known as behavioral change. We all attribute a good or bad habit to an event in the past. Some of these characters have a way of creating an effect in the body that suggests negatively towards achieving your goals. The causal factors of bad habits is often the effect of boredom and stress. When they take over your body, you are most likely to be affected both mentally and physically. The remoteness of bad habits cuts across all aspects in life, it may be as simple as impulse buying and as complex as engaging in a drinking spree.

The situation can change for the better. This will entail teaching yourself careful analysis of new methods that you can use in order to limit the effects of boredom and stress. This will entail seeking a substitute where you can channel them.

Sometimes the benefits follow the biological path like drinking and smoking. It can go ahead to be very emotional like when you stay in a relationship in which you are not happy. But, it may prevents you from feeling like you're isolated, and so you do it repeatedly. Because bad habits have some beneficial significance, it's very difficult to simply eradicate them from your routine. Instead, you embrace a new habit that provides a similar type of benefit in a bid to surpress the old habit. For example, if smoking eliminates your stress, and you know that smoking is not a good habit, the best remedy would be quit smoking. He habitual circle of replacement should be overcame by engaging in reproductive activities otherwise your needs remain unmet.

## Breaking the chain

In order to break this chain, you need to:

1. HAVE DESIRE TO QUIT/CHANGE THEM: Many people do not desire their bad habits to be removed. So you have to go very deep into your subconscious and demand to give it up. If you do, then move on to the next step.

2. HAVE A STRONG WILL POWER: Once you know what is going on, you need to act on it. Put your willpower into a motion and choose to change the bad habit. Remember it is your choice and only your choice. You are the only one who can change your life.

3. MAKE PLANS TO QUIT: Make a list, divide it into two columns, on the left, write down all that you know about your bad habits. Begin with the strongest one. On the right, find out the positive things you will require to get out of and write them down. Make connections between the negative habits and picturing yourself with the good things once you stopped the bad one.

4. TAKE ACTIONS: There are 2 ways of doing this. The first is to go for all or nothing or the second way is to start slow, taking small steps initially but working constantly or consistently toward your goal. Either way is OK, but choose what is good for you, as long as you reach your goal eventually.

5. SPEAK OUT: Tell someone you trust what you are doing and tell them your agenda. Have that person who asks you regularly about your progress, this will help you tremendously.

6. STOP, BUT DON'T TURN BACK: Almost impossible not to have setbacks. The major thing here is to get only setbacks and not turn backs. Keep going at it. Reset your goal for one more week and try again. If the week passes without setbacks, add another week.

7. REWARD YOURSELF: Always and regularly congratulate yourself if you have attained your objective by rewarding yourself with some stuff. It can be small victories for each step but plan and wait for a huge victory when you finally reach your goal and beat that bad habit.

Breaking bad habits requires time and effort, but mostly it takes consistency. Most people who end up breaking their bad habits try and failed multiple times before they make it work. You might not have success right away, but that doesn't mean you can't have it at all.

# What is mindfulness?

*Figure 3: Free Credits*

Mindfulness means bringing our full attention toward the present moment. We can also say that it a way of giving attention to our present thoughts and desires without judging them. The practice of mindfulness is written in Buddhist meditation. In recent years it enters America through the work of Jon Kabat-Zinn. His Mindfulness-Based Stress Reduction (MBSR) program is now being widely practiced in schools, prisons, veteran's center, etc. in America.

Mindfulness can be practiced by doing some following exercises-

- Pay attention- in this exercise we have to pay attention to every little detail of our present environment which we generally miss out like mild, touch, sound, sight, smell and taste.
- Focus on your breathing- breathing is an involuntary action and we generally don't give focus on it. Take deep breath to exhale out all your negative energies true breathing.
- Sitting meditation- sit comfortably with your back trait and closed. Breathe through your nose and focus on your breathing
- Walking meditation- find a place away from noise pollution and walked there for 10 to 20 minutes observing the beauty of nature.
- Accept yourself- treat yourself with kindness as you would treat a good friend of yours.

# Chapter 2: How your brain works

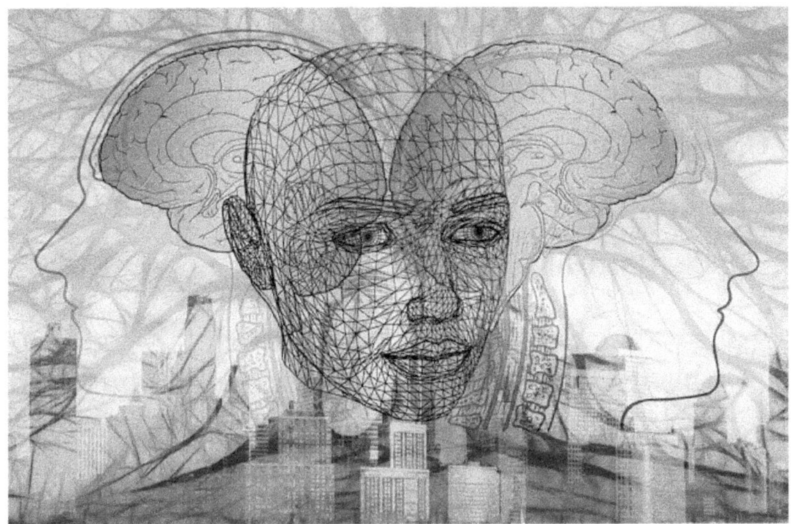

*Figure 4: Free Credits*

- **Conscious mind:** Consciousness means being fully aware of what's been going on around you and responding to it accordingly our conscious mind is practical and analytical. Conscious mind is has an important role in responding to the stimulus. It has no memory on its own and it can hold only one thought at a time. It identifies the information and passes the motor effect to our sense organs our body parts to take actions.

Conscious mind is also capable of comparing things. Certain memories stored in our subconscious mind are recorded by our conscious mind to compare the present situation with previous for another one. Moreover, our conscious mind can analyze think and make out conclusions from them. The most important function of a conscious mind that it helps in decision making.

- **Subconscious mind:** Our subconscious mind is in control of  all our involuntary actions and is a storehouse of thoughts emotions and feelings. Involuntary actions like heartbeat breathing rate peristalsis movement and function of organs are controlled by your subconscious mind. It also stores all the pieces of information it receives for a longer period then our conscious mind. Things which we do unknowingly are result of functioning of your subconscious brain like free don't feel that we are breathing unless we forcefully take it in our control, similarly we don't it no-no that we start to develop some feelings unless we take control over them with our conscious mind.

- **Working of amygdala:** Amygdala is a part of our limbic system located on each side of the temporal lobe. Amygdala takes care of the perception of emotion such as angle fear sadness and aggression. It stores memories of events and emotions so that we can relate to it when required in the future.  When the brain is turned upside down, where the structure ends continuous with the hippocampus is referred to as the uncus. Peeling away of the uncus exposes the amygdala which abuts the anterior of the hippocampus. Stimulation of the amygdala results to intense emotion such as aggression of fear. Irritative lessons of temporal lo epilepsy have the effect of stimulating the amygdala. When in extreme form, irritated lessons of temporal lobe epilepsy can lead to panic attack. Ablation causes an opposite effect to the Amygdala

- **Working of cortex:** The cerebral cortex is a thin layer covering an outer portion of the cerebrum and covered by meninges. Cerebral cortex is also referred to as grey matter because the nerves in this area are devoid of insulation that make most of the other part of the brain appear white. The cerebral cortex consists of furrows called sulci and bulges called gyri. It increases the surface area of the brain and the amount to grey matter is also increased. An increase amount of grey matter, increases the more the pieces of information can be processed. The cerebral cortex has both sensory and motor areas. Thalamus sends sensory signals to the sensory area to process information. The sensory area consists of the visual cortex of the occipital lobe, auditory cortex of the temporal lobe, gustatory cortex and the somatosensory cortex of the parietal lobe. There is a Association area which lies within the sensory area and gives meaning to the sensation by associating it with specific stimulus. The motor area includes primary motor cortex and premotor cortex which regulates voluntary movement.

The functions of cerebral cortex are-

1) Determination of Intelligence

2) Determination of personality

3) Conduction of motor functions

4) Planning and Organization

5) Processing sensory pieces of information

6) Processing language

7) Touch sensation

By doing research scientist relate the brain mechanism to behavioral function. A recent article describes how the visual cortex sees. The visual cortex area is made up of 6 main layers of the cell. This layer circuit of cell help to realize the process of learning development attention and 3D vision through a combination of horizontal, top-down and bottom-up interactions. The main aim of this experiment was to show how cortex region helps in learning and development.

# Chapter 3: Rewire your brain

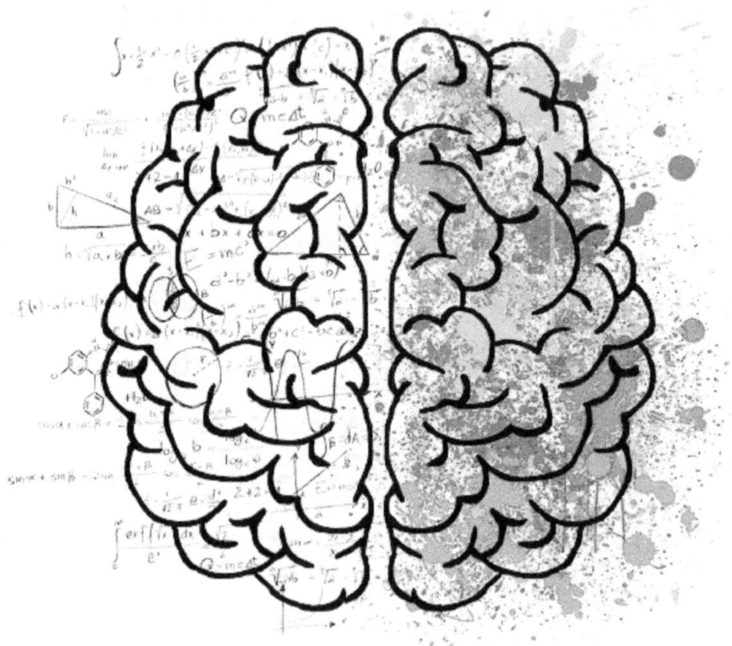

*Figure 5: Free Credits*

Our brain is ever-changing, dynamic and continuously reshaping itself concerning our environment, surroundings, people and information it perceives, however, our approach or our way to look at different things become static over time. Do you know why?

It all happens because of the paradigms that result from the old beliefs, ideology, religion, and dominant thoughts that we hold in our consciousness. The paradigm is the habitual way of thinking, and influence the way we look at things.

Rewiring your brain means restructuring the paradigm and perception to look at things, situations, and circumstances with a different approach. Most of the people in our time are living with a negative or lack paradigm, they focus on the negative or weaker aspects of every situation. The force behind this negative approach is Fear. But what is Fear?

Fear is simply seeing and expecting something will go wrong in the future. And as we expect, things do go wrong as all thoughts are working for it. By rewiring our brains; We try to approach an optimistic and hopeful way of looking at the things. But what is hope?

Hope is different from fear as its focus on faith that something beautiful is waiting for us in the future. Faith is expecting great things and patiently believing in the unseen. Both fear and hope works on something in the future, but what we choose is depending on our paradigm. The paradigm is not something that can be changed overnight, but for rewiring your brain the best time is now.

## Tips for rewiring your brain

We always keep thinking and dwelling about our past and future, as a result, we miss the things happening in our present. The present is the moment where your life is happening, and if we can clear our head, we can understand that it is the present moment that eventually become our past and our future. So learn to calm your mind, let go of the things that hold you back in your life. Try to become aware in the present moment because it is the time where all the creation is happening. All the things that we want will come out of this moment.

Rewiring of the brain means simplifying the complex process of decision making, evaluating different choices, rearranging the thought process. Calmness of mind gives greater freedom and joy in life by becoming of our thoughts.

Paradigm gives you a perception of everything around you like people, places, community, and religion. Our surroundings and neighborhood influence the mindset or belief we possess. A habit is something that we do regularly and in a similar manner. It reflects a person's choice and preferences. They are both Good and Bad habits. Good habits help us to enhance our skills, knowledge, and improve our health. Gym, Swimming, reading, and exercising are some of the habits that are considered as good habits as they add to our physical, emotional, and mental well-being. Things that adversely the functioning of our body and hamper our skills and productivity are bad habits. Something bad, unpleasant, harmful, or undesirable are bad habits. Whether it's not proper sleeping, lack of exercise, poor food choices, or drugs and alcohol addictions- we know these things are unhealthy for us.

We must understand that time is a non-renewable and limited. To gain something, we must let go of something. We can't have everything at once in life. We have to choose our focus and priorities.

- First of all, analyze your habits and then gradually bring up novel habits into your lifestyle.

- Engage them one at a time lest you want to lose focus of what is key.

- Priority is key when it comes to arranging them.

- It will take some time and commitment.

- Success is a continuous process

- Studies of the adult brain in recent decades has shown that changing the needs and experiences of an individual changes the way the brain functions. It was seen that the brain functionality halted at 30.

- The brain is a complex organ, despite massive achievements in how well we can comprehend and actualize the activity of the brain. It turnouts that we're still dwarfs in understanding about specific mechanisms.

- In times of  stress, the brain will take the less subtle path, and use as little energy as possible in decision making, so it'll revert to habits.

- Positive emotions are not the only ones that can rewire our brain, negative emotions like stress and anxiety can also have serious impacts.

- Training is required constantly to rewire the brain, it will enhances the ability to ignore irrelevant information that can result in hampered brain reaction to emotional events.

- Mindful meditation, travelling and staying as far away from stress as possible.

## EFT to address negative emotions and anxiety

EFT stands for Emotional Freedom Technique or Emotional Freedom Tapping. This technique addresses emotions as an adaptive experience caused by the settlement of feeling in the current environment. The main purpose of EFT technique is to release emotional anxieties through the energy pathways. This is a process where anxiety can be released by tapping on specific energy pathway position present on our body. I talk about it in depth in chapter 4.

## "Music can change the world because it can change people." - Bono

Classical music can improve memory, focus, and concentration. Soft instrumental ambient music can induce relaxed alertness. While whole-brain thinking is necessary for creativity and deeper insight, lyrics are found to compete for the brain's attention and decrease one's ability to concentrate and focus.

Powerful music with heavy tunes encourages deeper, abstract, and visionary thinking with an increased level of imaginary control- these are all attributes that are frequently associated with intellectually strong people. Music can help you get through hard times, enhance happy moments, and even teach you valuable life lessons. That is why musicians tend to have a different thinking and learning patterns, compared to people who just listen to music for killing boredom.

The whole research process has shown that music is directly connected to parts of the brain involved in decision making, paying attention, concentration, and memory. The part when the brain had the most activity were surprisingly the moments when there was silence in between music. Some people also claim that most beneficial activities when you play or listen to music.

# Exercise and rewiring the brain

*Figure 6: Free Credits*

There are plenty of good reasons to be physically active. The great ones are reducing the chances of developing heart diseases, stroke, and diabetes. Exercise and physical workout lower your blood pressure, increases the flow of oxygen, prevent depression. It protects memory and thinking skills. The benefits of physical workout come directly from its ability to reduce insulin resistance, reduce inflammation, and stimulate the release of growth of new blood vessels in the brain, and even the recovery and survival of new brain cells.

Exercise improves health and sleep, and can reduce stress and anxiety. It affects the brain on multiple fronts. It increases heart rate, which pumps more oxygen to the brain and provides a nourishing environment for the growth of brain cells.

Aerobic exercise is great for body and brain: not only does it improve brain function, but it also acts as a first aid kit on damaged cells.

Exercising spike brain activity and prepare for mental stresses. It increases retention of new information, and better reaction to complex situations. Both aerobic and resistance training had benefited to cognitive function.

Exercise may help lift your mood in some milder cases, Depression slows the brain's ability to process information, makes it more difficult for us to focus and reach decisions. Exercise cranks up the body's production of serotonin and dopamine, brain chemicals crucial to happiness.

Exercise improves cognitive abilities like being able to focus on complex tasks, to think rightly, to organize, and to plan for future events.

People who exercise regularly tend to do so because it gives them an enormous sense or state of well-being. They feel more energetic throughout the day, sleep better at night, feel more relaxed and positive about themselves, and have sharper memories.

Regular exercise is an investment in your mind, body, and soul. It can foster your sense of self- worth and make you feel relaxed and strong.

Exercise activates growth-stimulating proteins in the brain that may help form new cells there.

## Better sleep and rewiring the brain

- Sleep does more than help us recover from stress and tiredness it rewires the brain, shutting down during the night allows the body to produce new synapses which connect brain cells.

- Neurologists think the creation of new synapses is one key way the brain encodes memories and learning, but that it cannot go on indefinitely without a rest.

- Most people pay little attention to directing their thoughts. Most people believe that you have to think whatever thought pops up in your brain, whether you like it or not.

- When you exercise a muscle, you make it strong. When you exercise a thought, you make it dominant. You exercise a thought, you think it over and over, repetitively.

- Replace the dominant fearful thoughts with neutral, calm, boring thoughts repetitively and make them dominant.

- Thoughts of failure, for instance, puts our brain in touch with an infinite number of negative neural connections in our head that leads to stress.

- What matters is what you choose to focus on before you go to bed, before your subconscious plays with your most powerful thoughts experiences for eight hours.

- Include habits that relax you and releases stress and anxiety. Try reading, listening to calm music, stretching, meditation, a cup of tea, anything that puts in the mood for slumber.

Rewiring the brain for happiness

- Our brains are wired to negative, but the good news is that you can train your mind to hold on to happiness in a few moments a day.

- We can train our brain to scan for the good things in life to help you see more possibility, to feel more energy and to succeed at higher levels.

- And once we make that internal shift, we can put our daily external frustrations into perspective.

- It is proven, when we raise the positivity levels in our brain, we actually do better work and, generally, are happier.

- Our brain continuously scans for bad news, when he finds the bad news, it overly focuses on it.

- "The brain is like a garden, except its soil is very fertile for weeds,"- Hanson

- "Showing gratitude for all the good things we have in our life attracts abundance, positivity, and love."

- Gratitude has been linked to a host of physical and psychological benefits, including happiness.

- Counting the blessings, luck, fortunes, and everything good that happened in your today makes us grateful, affirmative, and optimistic in life.

Focusing on the good isn't just about overcoming our inner grump to see the glass half full. It's about opening our minds to the ideas and opportunities that will help us become more productive, effective, and successful at work and in life.

# Chapter 4: The EFT technique

*Figure 7: Free Credits*

## Basic approach to EFT technique

It is a form of psychological acupressure based on the same energy meridian used in traditional acupuncture to clear out all the energy disturbances in the meridian but without the use of needles. It is a simple tapping process where fingertips is used to input kinetic energy onto specific meridian on head and chest while you think about your specific problem whether it is an event, an addiction, illness or happiness. This method has been successfully used to treat war veterans that have undergone various forms of trauma including post-traumatic stress disorder. This is despite the fact that the method is still being researched. There are a few factors that needs to be considered before beginning the procedure.

What is the issue?

First of all, you need to identify the cause of anxiety, trauma or any other stress which the patient is suffering from. You also need to evaluate the nature of the problem and the amount of damage it has caused. This will determine the most appropriate approach to treatment using EFT. Keep in mind that you can only address one problem at a time. It has been proven that focusing on one problem at a time improves the chances of recovery as compared to focusing on multiple problems at a go.

What is the initial intensity of the issue?
This gives you an opportunity to monitor progress in the course of EFT treatment. The initial intensity can be measured on a scale of 0 to 10. If the test results are approaching zero, it means there is tremendous improvement and that you are respond will to the treatment. Values close to 10 means the improvement is not satisfactory. You will need to be a little more aggressive and focus on different sports while performing the sequence. Also set targets and goals for every sequence. This helps you come up with a benchmark with which to measure your progress after each sequence.

The setup

After you have identified the issue and tested its initial intensity, it is now time to put up a set up for the procedure. First, you need to prepare yourself physically, mentally, and emotionally for the whole thing. Accept that you have the problem and that you are ready to tackle it at that moment. You also need to accept yourself in that condition and aspire to become a better person after the procedure. Acknowledging the issue and accepting yourself are the first two steps towards recovery. It sets your attitude and mindset towards treatment. Try comparing how the problem makes you feel to how relieving you from the problem will make you feel. Remaining with it might disturb you forever but treating it will last just a few weeks or months and you are free again.

## How EFT works

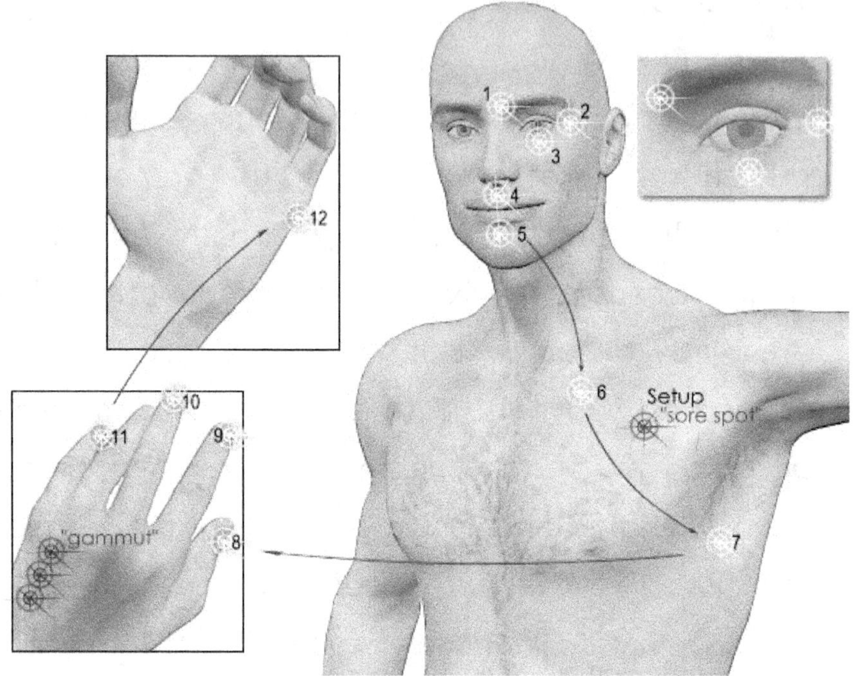


*Figure 8: Free Credits*

All negative emotions are caused by disturbances in our body's energy system. There are 14 energy pathways to our body which are called meridians. Disturbance in one or more of the energy meridians can cause negative emotions like anger, sadness, regret or shame. The technique is based on Chinese traditional medicine and works in the same way as acupuncture. The only difference being that EFT uses fingertips to tap energy instead of needles. The tapping occurs on energy hotspots throughout the body such as eyes, nose, chin, collarbone, all the way down to other spots. The tapping should be procedural, starting from the top and moving downwards.

- In this technique, a patient tries to focus on his negative thinking caused by any circumstances. He should have the realization that he is having some negative thoughts in his head.
- Then the patient tabs on a set of 10 meridian point rather than 14 because some of the energy points are intersection of two acupressure pathways so tapping on only 10 it creates an impact of tapping or 14 of them

- These tapping technique releases all the blockages in our energy meridian. At first hour negative energies seems intense but gradually hit trains down and vanishes.

The Following are The Tapping Points on Our Body

- Top of the head- to find this meridian, stuck your thumb into your ears and raise your other four fingers straight up in the air and lie it down top of your head. Or generally look straight and tap with four fingers on top of your head to release anxiety.
- Between your eyebrows and diesel cartilage diesel- there are two energy points on either side of the nasal cartilage on the beginning of eyebrows. Use two fingers to tap in between your eyebrows, at the beginning of one eyebrow. Fingers should be slightly tilted down towards the nasal cartilage.
- On the side of the eye- it is present at the end of the eyebrow on the bony socket of eye. The corner of the eye is called the side of the eye point.

- Below the eye- it lies write down the iris in the bony socket of eye (not on the cheekbone). Use two fingers to tap on it by keeping one finger near elevation of a nose and one beside it.

- Under the nose point- it is present right below the nose and above the lip, right in the middle.

- On the chin point- it lies below the lower lip and above the chin in little valley right in the middle.

- Between collarbones- there is a U shaped depression between the collar bones. the tapping point lies there. Use your closed fist to tap there.

- Below armpits- It does not lie in the armpits but below it. Man can find it by aligning his hand along with nipple to below armpit and women can find it right where there is their bra strap below arm. Tap with all four fingers under your arm.

- Wrist point - there is a line where your wrist joins your arm, put your three fingers on that line, you will find the tapping point below the third finger.

- Side of wrist point- on side of your wrist below the pinky finger lies the tipping point in between the edge of your wrist.

- How you tap on this point doesn't matter, what is important is that you should find the right place to tap. You can try several places in a systematic manner. Pay attention to how you feel when a spot is touched. After identifying the spot that gives more relief, concentrate on it for some minutes.

Test the Final Intensity

After you have performed the EFT sequence to your satisfaction, measure the results in the same scale of 0 to 10 and see where you stand. Compare this with the test results you came up with in the initial testing. If the results are at zero, then you have done well. Anything less than zero is an indication that you will need to either make minor change or re-do the whole process.

## How to hack your mind to beat anxiety: 15 points

*Figure 9: Free Credits*

## 1. By EFT technique:

In this process of combination of tapping energy and voice thing positive formation works to clear the emotional block from our mind. This to in combination sensors positive bioenergy to restore our mind and body balance. How to hack your mind to beat anxiety E and become strong against it

## 2. Take deep breaths:

Whenever you feel anxious just stop for a moment and just close your eyes for some moment and take Deep breaths it releases much of the nervousness through breathing out. It has been proven very effective in releasing stress.

### 3. Convince your brain that you are strong:

The most common reason for being anxious is nervousness. Tackle your mind to convince it that you are in a safe situation and you need not to be nervous or fearful about it. Talk to yourself what are you so so weak ok that any situation can feel you with anxiousness. Always give a positive answer to yourself that you are strong and nothing can make you stressed.

### 4. Read motivational Books:

Whenever you can't find peace in your mind and nothing is helping you to get out of your anxiety, read motivational books. It contains a lot of life experiences and examples which helps us to recognize ourselves. It brings out the hidden happy soul in us which discovered by Bhaihe worries.

5. Change your environment:

Our environment affects us a lot in every way. If you don't feel comfortable and nervous in your environment for example if you are feeling uncomfortable between a group of people then leave or if you are feeling doubtful a thing don't accept it. Changing your environment can change your present situation of mind and can prevent you from being anxious.

6. Cut down on caffeine:

Too much caffeine can also make you anxious because caffeine affects our mind and make it more active. Consuming too much of it makes our mind restless and our mind always Desire Tu to do something even while we are resting. This might affect our sleep and meditation which can make us stressed. When you are feeling that you are anxious don't consume a lot of caffeine. Calm down your mind by having some water or juice.

7. Mediate:

Meditation helps in gaining concentration bye only focusing on one point at a time. When you close your eyes a lot of thoughts come into your mind. In meditation, we focus only on one goal to keep to be e accomplished at a time. It helps in gaining an enormous amount of courage to do that task do meditation every morning for at least 10 minutes to focus on your goals and achievements. Find a quiet and clean environment to do your meditation. Make it last as long as you it makes you comfortable. Also make it consistent, an everyday habit.

8. Treat yourself:

Treat yourself with some reward even if you feel anxious. This shows your positive attitude even if you are stressed out. The energies of Your subconscious mind filled with negativity collide with the energies of positivity of conscious action and revert. Keep your conscious actions always positive to fight from all the negativity field in here conscious subconscious part.

9. Take a shower:

Taking a shower cleans away your aura, do it might be filled with positivity or negativity. Your which body and soul comes out as a wait mud which can be e shape into any form. So so as you to come out of shower see the world as a beautiful place and fill your mind with the thought that you love your life.

10. Indulge yourself in some other work:

If you work monotonously on a single task your mind might become dull and depressed. Our mind is very complex it contains a lot of neurons which are are active at different times, remaining on a single task stresses out only one part of the brain while other parts remain inactive. So don't do the same work for hours, give rest to your active part of your brain and use other parts bye doing different works.

11. Don't be hungry and Sleepless:

If you remain hungry and Sleepless your mind will only Crave for food and sleep. Work as per your routine without overstressing yourself. Neither take long breaks from work nor work for a longer period. Neither starve in the craze of work nor sleep much in your break have a balance in everything you do. in this way you can keep every part of your brain active at some time. Keep in mind that lack of sleep hinders your brain's ability to think. Studies show that 95 percent of the wrong decisions we make is as a result of either not getting enough sleep or having irregular sleeping patterns. When the brain is ide is when negative and unstable thoughts start streaming into our minds and polluting our thoughts. Food is the source of nourishment for the brain. Lack of enough energy slows down the activities of the brain and might even be fatal. Even if your appetite is low, force something down your throat for the sake of other parts like the brain. You don't have to eat your usual mountain of food at a go, break down your eating intervals to up to six times a day. Eat little by little until you achieve your daily ratio.

12.    Don't sit at one place for a long time:

Sitting in one position for longer time fatigues your muscles. You can get muscle cramps when you stand up. Our veins get jammed and blood flow ceases temporarily in some parts of our body when we are sitting in a fixed position for a certain period. As soon as you change your position blood start to flow in that part of the body which was being pressed while you were sitting. Every cell in our body needs oxygen to oxidize food which it gets from blood. Temporary ceasing of blood supply to some parts of our body can cease the function of cells. So don't sit in one posture for prolonged time and change your position even when you are sleeping.

13. Wear the clothes which makes you feel happy and confident:

Social anxiousness can be caused by the feeling of getting commented on. If you don't feel comfortable in your body your mind cannot let go away the fear of being judged. So wear the clothes you feel comfortable in without working on what people say. Remember that it is all about you and not anyone else. There is no point in pleasing other people while you are actually hurting and feeling uncomfortable from the outside.

14.    Talk to your mother:

Science has proven that talking to your mother release this anti-stress hormone. Your mother is the only person who cares about you. You are a part of the body so remain close to her. Even seen her face releases much of our anxiety. Whenever you feel lo, talk to your mother or just sit beside her. She always has a good desire for us and her positive Vibes attracts you and drains away your stress.

15.    Comb your hair and massage your body:

Anxiety affects both our mind and body. Our head feels heavy when we are filled with stress. Combing your hair can increase your blood circulation makes your mind active charges your brain with electrons (which are charge carriers) and releases stress. Our body feels heavy dull and painful when we are too anxious, massage your body according to ayurvedic process and let all the negative energies drain down and come out of your toe. Make this an everyday habit, don't wait to get stressed up before combing your hair. Always massage parts of your body that you'd like them massaged. Don't do it as a punishment, just do it randomly anytime your hands are free. Twist your neck by holding the back of your head with both hands every time you keep it in the same position for long. Crack your knuckles and massage the joints of your fingers as you wait for someone.

# Chapter 5: Natural Medicines: Rewiring negativity into positivity

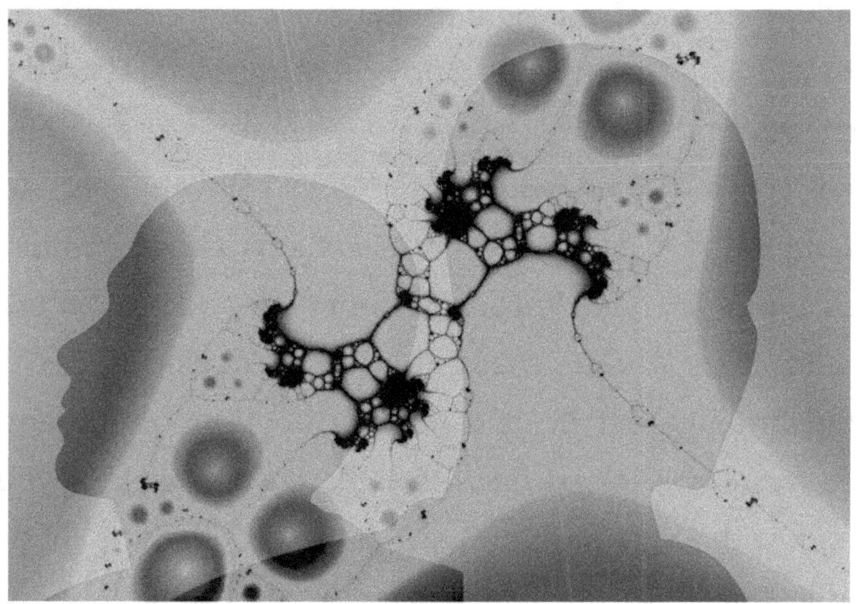

*Figure 10: Free Credits*

## Mirror neuron

Mirror neurons are the neurons that show action in both conditions when a person does an action or observe others doing that the basic function of mirror neurons is that it helps in understanding actions that are done by others. It is a small circuit of cells present in the premotor cortex and the inferior parietal cortex. It is called mirror neurons because as mirror reflects us and ID whatever actions we do in front of it, in the same way mirror neurons shoe action when it sees others doing the same thing. These neurons are well studied in primitive species like monkeys. You might have seen some real-life examples of Monkey copying you and thought that the monkey is doing it just for fun, but the real fact is that there are mirror neurons are active when they see people doing activities.

We people have a more developed mind then animals. We have our Desire thoughts unwillingness to do a thing so power motor neurons are not so active and we don't the things by seeing others. But we are the evolved species of the primate monkeys so how can we not copy others. Do we have self-control still we sometimes tend to lose it and start copying other people which in some way is good and also bad. We should only copy others regarding the things which are beneficial for us and which can improve us to be a better person, like learning good manners from others. There is no harm in following other good qualities to make our life better.

Mirror neurons as Natural healers

The other group of neurons which get triggered by its environmental stimulus. Our environment affects us teaching us thanks a lot of things may it be having pros or cons. Mirror neurons have a great impact on honor learning and emotions. They can also show actors natural healers because it absorbs us into our environment. Whenever you feel anxious to be in a positive environment and around people who make you happy.

Effect of mirror neurons in our brain:

- Effect on our learning: Mirror neurons play a critical role in human abilities like speech habits language behavior etc. Because of our mirror neurons, we learn actions by seeing others even though they are not being taught to us. The memory of observed actions is stored in the subconscious mind and are executed by mirror neurons for output. Like if we are around a group of people who are eating our mind also directs us to eat even though our stomach might be full. We start to learn things by induction and implement them in our life. For example, middle Eastern countries observe the culture and tradition of Western countries and implement them in their life do they are not being taught by western peoples.

- Effect on our emotions: Emotional recognition and empathy is been linked to Mirror neurons. Association between mirror neurons and emotions have been shown by fMRI scans. This has observed the imitation of facial expression based on emotion. when two individuals interact there emotional States effects each other. Like you can't be happy when you're your dear ones are sad. Being happy and inducing happiness to others is the effect of mirror neurons activated in our brain.

## Listen to each other

Share your part of sadness and misery can actually decrease the low emotional feeling in you. By sharing your grief you let out all the negative energies from the body. Talking and listening to each other can be a natural healer as you feel that you are not alone in your life. Being connected to someone makes it easy to run the errands of life. Which has been proven by psychologists that Having a conversation with your partner can clean your Aura. Communication gap can create a crack in a relationship. Even if you have any conflict for the misunderstanding with your partner talk and listen to each other this is the only way to dissolve the barriers between you. Having conversation Tu to decrease your differences doesn't mean Tu To overpower your partner by showing anger and superiority. Only by giving them equal place in your heart and mind your distances can be turned into closeness.

# Friendship

*Figure 11: Free Credits*

Friends are companions who do not let us feel lonely. We become friends with a person only when our thoughts match. Being with someone so much like you makes you feel happy at first place. You have so many things in common to talk about regarding your studies daily life fashion sense your other friends and a lot more. We become close to our friends and share everything because we don't have the fear that they will judge us. We cannot be friends with our parents because there is an age an experience gap between us and also their superiority and fear of being judged makes us feel nervous before sharing our feelings.

Friends are the most important part of our childhood and it is the age when we are shaping our mind to become a intellectual person. As we spend half of our childhood in schools and colleges we are mostly around our behavior and nature has a great impact on us. Therefore we should choose our friend wisely on whom we can rely on. We should not break our friendship with old friends because they were part of our ups and downs. When we grow old we don't remember how much money we have earned but we do remember power memories with our friends.

Advantages of having friends-

- Friends help you in your problems
- They don't judge you easily
- You can have trust on them and keep your heart out
- They are the storehouse of Laughter medicine
- Cherishing old memories with your friends makes your mind nostalgic and sharp
- When you see your friends anti-stress hormone releases from our endocrine system
- You can call a friend for any suggestions and advice

# Chapter 6: Can your brain rewire itself?

*Figure 12: Free Credits*

## How to stop worrying

Bad habits such as worrying can be turned into a catalyst that keeps you energized and productive. Actually, it's possible with a little help from the way we think.

Worry normally puts you into a state of guilt, regret or getting stuck in the past or things that may happen in the future. we may worry about everything – from our current financial state to the weather or anything that affects our lifestyle.

Worry normally has two results – productivity and unproductivity. The unproductive worry is that on which we have no control over. For example, you may be worried about any natural catastrophe. There's nothing you can do about it, so it's a waste of time and to worry about it.

Productive worry involves a situation you can control, such as your examination. In case you haven't studied enough to pass a week before the exam and you sit on the couch and start worrying about passing or failing. Besides wasting your time in unnecessary thinking make plans for studying and take action for it.

The truth about worry:

Generally, worry and guilt is a virtually useless emotion. It does have a small purpose i.e. it focuses on possible problems that you may be able to prevent before they intensify. Personally, I would define it as concern rather than worry. It becomes worried when you let it get worse and you keep thinking about what could go wrong.

If you immediately take action on your concern; your concern will provide some benefit. However, the major problem arises when you remain affected by it for a longer period i.e. you become worried; either about possible problems that you have not acted on or, possible problems which you cannot do anything to curb.

You have to empty your mind of all negative thoughts before you can become productive. To clear your mind write down your worries and analyze them. Your anxiety will likely recede when you can focus only on the task at a time, and removing the mess from your mind.

As you begin to control your worry patterns and work through them, you'll build flexibility so that you can face future circumstances with confidence. You'll begin to see that when you avoid situations you're worried about (such as examination), the situation only becomes worse.

The most important factor in dealing with worry is to deal with it at the first opportunity, preferably while it can still be defined as concern. The next step is to write down your concern/worries on a paper where you can deal with it.

After you complete this five-step process, your productivity will improve because you will no longer be wasting time worrying about things which you can do nothing about. You will also be free from your remaining worries by taking positive and corrective action to deal with them. This frees up your mental resources to work on important tasks while reducing your stress levels.

Worry is one of the most common signs of stress:

Learn to transform your worry into productivity, when you master this technique, you'll be amazed at how you can mentally pull yourself out of a stressful situation and get back to solving the stressful situation reasonably and logically. Too many people think that worry can be avoided and ignored but if you try to take that loom, your worries will grow intense as your deadline comes closer. You will always have worries for which you can do nothing about. You simply have to accept the fact and leave these worries in the hands of destiny. The key to dealing with worry is learning to realize when it starts to enter your mind. You can use the above-mentioned process to fight from worries.

## How to stop feeling feared

Fear is the worst feeling in our lives. All these fears of what will happen which does not exist at present make us paralyzed. There are many people who cannot take any big step for fear. So in order to achieve our success, we have to avoid fear. If our society cannot overcome fear, then it will become a problem. Especially if our young society gets frightened by it then fear will spread all over the world. So we have to get out of fear.

Types of Fear:

1. Psychological Fear: Emotional fear is the biggest fear of human life. Fear is never present. what'll happen? This is the root cause of fear. It is dangerous if you leave the present and move into the future. If you can live in the present, there will be no fear in your life. Mental Fear Like this fear if you have the ability to do something, you cannot do it for emotional fear. We can see that man can do many things but his fear does not allow him to do so.

2. Physical Fear: Physical fear is normal. Physical phobia You often have nothing to do. Suppose you did that to a tiger, then you must be scared. And if you're not scared then you have to go get a tiger. So it is necessary to have physical fear. Physical fear can come to you in any way. Be prepared for it. Physical fear is never said.

Fear is something we develop within ourselves by gaining things that can harm us. A kid doesn't fear anything. Do you know the reason why kids don't fear anything? It is because they have fewer emotions than we have. And they have fewer emotions because of a lack of information about the real world.

Life is full of ups and downs while growing up we learn a lot of things. As we gather information we take it in a positive as well as negative way. So getting back to your question, if you are fearful about everything then it means that you have a lot of information about everything. Think by yourself that "is it good?".

Absolutely no. You have a lot of information about everything but it is stored in a wrong sense. You have to overcome this fear. Well, there might be a few things which can help you out:

1. "Failure is the pillar to success". Whoever said this is absolutely correct. You know what your actual fear is? It is fear of failure. If you succeed continuously, you shall gradually be used to it and when you face failure for the first time, it would be very difficult for your brain to accept the fact. So if you ask what should be done, I would suggest that fail sometimes and make mistakes ( which doesn't cost you a life) and learn from them as they are your best teachers.

2. Get out of your comfort zone. Well it is as difficult as it sounds. Fight your fear. Fight it as if you are in a war. It is the biggest war because it is between 2 hemispheres of your brain. Make mistakes, laugh at yourself, enjoy the moment you live.

3. If you find it difficult to be fearless, act as if you do not fear anything. Act with full confidence. In this way you can improve yourself.

4. Think about yourself and not what others think of you. It is your life, not theirs.

5. Learn from people you meet or see and try to find out what their fear is and how they deal with it. Not only it gives you confidence but also it makes you courageous to face similar kind of fear.

6. Fear is normal. Every person has some kind of fear but most of the people do not show it and act like a fearless person. So, remember you are not the only one.

7. Make good friends and share your fears or life experiences with them. This way you shall not feel insecure or alone most of the time.

So the way to overcome this fear is to be truthful to yourself and others as well, just keep doing the right things at the right time, don't get carried away while in distress and commit mistakes.

Danger is for real but fear is a product of our thoughts. Fear is just a choice that we rather get horrified from a situation or face it fearfully.

# Importance of sleep well

*Figure 13: Free Credits*

Sleep has a vital role in good health and a healthy mind throughout your life. It is very important to get enough sleep at the right time to protect your mental health and physical health.

While you sleep your brain supports your physical and mental health. If you don't get enough sleep or sleep at the wrong time or sleep restlessly, you will feel dizzy when you wake up.

Following are the reasons why good sleep is important:

1. Good sleep keeps your heart healthy:

- Lack of sleep has been associated with worsening of blood pressure and cholesterol, which can lead to strokes and other heart diseases. This is because our mind and body don't get enough time to rest, and it ultimately affects our heart health.
- Heart problems are already killing millions in the world. The least we can do is avoid the risk factors for the same. For that, you need to get at least 7-9 hours of sleep every night.

2. Good sleep can help you lose weight:

- Researchers have shown that people who get fewer hours of sleep are mostly because Poor sleep quality or lack of sleep directly affects our digestive system and appetite, making us eat more calories

- But if you sleep early and well, your calories burn faster and your appetite stays healthy, decreasing your calorie intake.

3. Good sleep can increase your chances of success:

- Shocking, right? Not really. Sleep is important for various brain functions like cognition, concentration, productivity, and performance. Our memory improves when we have a deep, quality sleep. All these factors play a very important role in determining your chances of success. So, don't stay up late trying to focus on something for hours, have a good night sleep and it will be easy for you to learn things easily in fewer hours.

4. Good sleep can decrease chances of diabetes:

- Sleep quality affects our blood sugar levels, deprivation in sleep can cause pre-diabetes in healthy adults in as little as six days. If people adopt a healthy sleeping pattern, they can avoid the risk of this disease even though it's there in their ancestral family.

- If you already have diabetes, avoid experimental sleeping patterns and take proper rest to avoid the risk.

## 5. Good sleep can help you with anxiety & stress:

- When your body is sleep deficient, it goes into a state of stress as it is trying to be on high alert. Fewer hours of sleep can also increase your anxiety levels and can cause more and more mental health issues.
- Good sleeping habits can relieve your stress and anxiety while you're asleep, draining the negative energy. When you get a really good sleep sometimes, you feel refreshed and energetic in the morning. It's all because of a good night sleep!

## 6. Good sleep strengthens your immune system:

- Sleep is a time to relax, but it's also a time during which the body is working hard to repair the damage caused by stress, ultraviolet rays, and other harmful exposure. This repairing and constant healing strengthens our immune system, reducing the risks of almost all diseases. On the other hand, even the smallest loss of sleep can make your immune system more prone to diseases, and can make you catch cold, viral fever etc. quite frequently.

7. Bad sleep is linked to inflammation:

- Stress hormones are released more when we don't get enough sleep which can raise the levels of inflammation in our body. It damages our cells and increases inflammation until it becomes a big problem for your health.
- Let our bodywork naturally i.e. give it appropriate time to sleep and rest so that it can slowly decrease inflammation (if we have it).

8. Good sleep may help prevent cancer:

- Researchers have linked colon and breast cancer to poor sleep quality. People who work all night and compromise on their rest are more likely to develop these cancers. This happens because light exposure reduces melatonin levels – a hormone that regulates the sleep-wake cycle.

This hormone protects against cancer, suppressing the growth of tumors. Eating healthy and exercising are known to be the pillars of a long & healthy life, but until now, you were unknown to another pillar without which the roof can fall – good sleep.

## How affirmations and mantras help to rewire your brain?

Affirmations are intensely personal, which means different ones will work better for different people. The biggest question arises is that does your intention speak to your soul? Don't try to do something that will not benefit you in any way. Listen to yourself and you'll begin to know what kind of affirmations you need the most.

Following are some way to practice your affirmation every day-

- Practice subliminal affirmation: Busy life we don't have much time to think about the affirmations we should carry out. But we can make some efforts to practice affirmations by having self talk. We can talk to ourselves why we are doing any work like cooking driving studying or Surfing the internet. The subliminal affirmations make their way into our minds without the knowledge of our consciousness. You can also listen to some soothing music which absorbs positive affirmations from the vibrations created by buying the music.

- News Technology to have a hand on your affirmations: You can use your mobile phone to record the affirmations you want to practice and set a reminder so that you can be reminded of it every once in a while. You can even record it in your own voice and listen to it.

- Visualize your affirmation in your mind: by visualizing pieces of information you will have a clear image of your goal in your head. Like if you are performing to lose weight imagine yourself as a slim person and the dress you wanted to buy but you couldn't because of your weight. This will help you to motivate yourself to complete your affirmation.

- Write down your affirmations: The easiest way you have a grab on all your affirmations is to write it down in your diary which you use every day. In this way you can have a handy way of carrying all your operations wherever you go so that you can practice your affirmations 10 times daily.

# Chapter 7: 100 Positive Affirmations

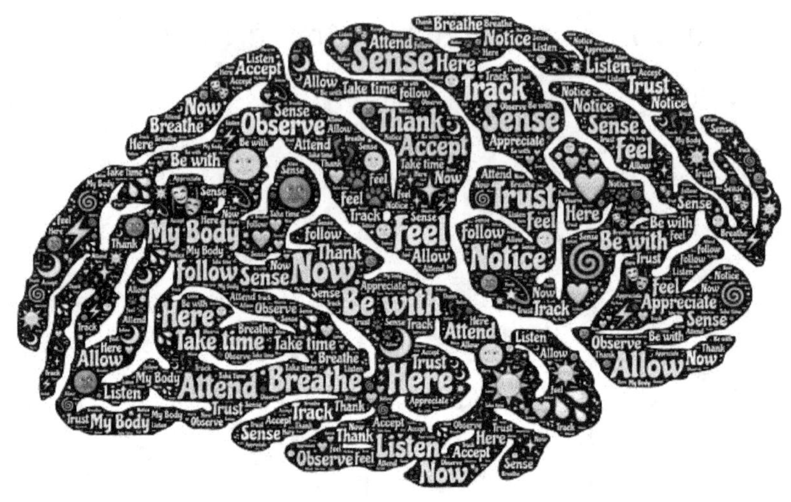

*Figure 14: Free Credits*

Following are the 100 positive affirmations which can be practiced everyday effortlessly without any hassle. The statements follow these topics: stop procrastination, more productivity, stop overeating, eat better, health, stop chronic disorganization, have a life more organized, staying in bad situations with more calm and awareness, stop excessive anxiety and worrying, Self-Medication, Self-Control, freeing yourself from mindless guilt, more confidence, rapid weight loss, health habits and more success.

1. Always stay positive

The key to success lies in one's positive state of mind even in failure. Keeping the mindset to win helps in overcoming all the misery. It encourages you to do your work without failing. A positive mind is always free from anxiety, discouragement, and fear it builds up your personality that lasts for long. Finding something good in every bad situation helps to keep your mind light and away from stress. I remain a positive person can easily recover from disease, is mind send positive Vibes to all over his body which helps him to cure. If you to create a positive Aura around you then negative energy and people will remain away from you. Your positive attitude is reflected outside as your confidence, boldness fearlessness.

2. Build up concentration

One of the very important aspect of leading a disciplined life is concentration. Whatever you are doing at that moment, have total focus on it. Work done in full concentration is more productive than doing it haphazardly. It is another key to success other than staying positive. It builds up a strong mind, willpower and self-control. Once a person determines to do the thing and gives his full concentration, the word behind him is model and no one can ever disturb him. Identify all potential distractions and lock them off. If it is friends that are hindering your concentration, let them know that you need some privacy. If they won't listen, cut them off altogether.

3. Learn from your failures

Failures are a test and trail of life, never be afraid to fail. The strongest people we have today have failed more times that you can imagine. It has its advantages and disadvantages. U need to extract out the advantage from your misery. Find a way through problems. You should not take failure as your weakness rather it's a phase for you to self-evaluate your mistakes and lacking's to overcome them. Whenever you are in an adversity ask yourself what has got me here and how can I get out of it what can I learn from it. If you to overcome this discomforts you will emerge as strong nature and a wise person Tu problem can break

4. Have patience

Patience is a gift which is confined to some persons. It's a unique power to sandal handle situations in a calm manner without being impulsive and showing anger. Don't do actions in anger and don't take decisions in excitement. Impulsive actions can result in adversity. Don't jump directly to conclusions think mindfully before you speak or do something. Bad words are like sword they can harm a person's sentiments which can later lead you to regret. Ginning patience build a strong mind and will power which can resist bad situations failure tragedies and can help you to overcome them. Work hard and have patience for your fruit. Don't be anxious bye impatiently worrying about the results.

5. Be updated

In today's world of competition if we don't level up with the technology and tradition can be left Behind and get crunched under the feet of development. The world changes every minute and it's the law of nature. Associate yourself with the people that are conscious of time. Time is always different a person, before 10 years you might be e a child Auron teenager who was doing different studies a work at that time after 10 years as you are in adult you have to take responsibility of your work ok your decisions and your life. You might be not the same person as you were before you feeling changes your body changes your liking changes and your way of living changes your relationship changes because nothing is is permanent in this world. Learn to move on from the trivial means of working and thinking and try to adapt your present surroundings. Detaching from past and living in the present makes you happy E and positive. Things changes only for your betterment So Be flexible in learn to adapt changes rather than opposing them.

6. Have a life more organized

Planning your day and work prevents you from wasting time .your day should be organized according to what things you have to get done in a certain period of time. Sometimes our subconscious mind overpowers our conscious mind and we just waste timeline daydreaming and assuming to get our work done. It's actually e a sign of weak mind which only assumes of doing work rather than taking action towards it. Your day should not be spent in doing random things; focus on things which really matters in present rather than having subconscious Desire of future

A Messy room messes up with our mind. Keep your things in an organized manner, it makes you easy to find your kinds of stuff at the time of usage. Don't put unnecessary things at your place, it's just a waste of money and space. Your environment should be airy, most of it's up space where air should be accommodated and create a suffocating environment. Try to keep you're your Ru in a light shade and shoes less printed ambiance (it gives Illusion of a less Messy room even though you have a lot of things). Keep things around you which gives you positive Vibes and disposes away the things which irritate you. Buying unnecessary things creates more waste which harms our nature.


7. Don't depend on luck

Destiny is based on Karma. A person's best deeds make his present and present deeds will make his future. We should not blame our luck because we are fully responsible for what we are today. Our attitude towards our life will build our future. Everything is in control of our will power that how much hard work we are doing to make our life better. Every day is not the same, if you are having success you can also have failure, if you are happy today you can be sad tomorrow, that doesn't mean that you have bad luck. If you feel helpless at a certain point in your life surrender yourself to the divine God and ask for help. He decides our destiny based on what we do. By having a positive attitude towards life and making actual physical actions we can fight against hurdles and obstacles that come through our way.

8. Stay away from negativity

Negative Vibes can create anxiety and depression so stay away from people who are negative about you your thoughts and your work. Don't hear comments and advice which discourages you. Negative people spread negativity because they have malice in the heart that if they can't do a thing why should others do it. Negativity in mind can refrain a person from accepting things respecting others and being positive towards the changes in life. If our minds are filled with negativity, it reflects in our personality and a negative aura is created around us which keeps away happiness and enjoyment from entering our conscious mind.

9. Stop overreacting

Overreacting is N impulsive action we do it without thinking much of the consequences thereafter. Taking everything too seriously and reacting much towards it creates anger and anxiety. Hair our subconscious mind overpowers our conscious mind and we e unnecessarily start imposing our thoughts on others. Our conscious mind makes us liberal and adjustable to the environment but the subconscious mind wants everything in its own way. Overreacting can do no good but can lead to future regret so before being impulsive at a point think twice whether it is of such importance to be reacted upon, if not then just ignore it. Everything can be done by keeping your mind calm and making understand your point to others. Words have more powers then emotions, so rather being emotional and reactive be a calmer person that can shape the world with his wisdom.

10. Take a break

The most effective way of working or studying is to do your job in full concentration for a fixed period of time and then take a break to relax your mind. Working monotonously and haphazardly for hours can make you dull and your work ok might remain incomplete. While doing a task just have focus on it let the world do their own work and you be busy in your own business until you take a break. In your leisure time, you can go out somewhere talk to friends, listen to music have some drinks eat something or you may watch something. Science has proven that taking a nap during daytime or between long hours of study can strengthen your brain, relaxes your body, fills you with confidence and lighten up your mood. People working in an office on a computer often tend to have headaches due to pressure in their eyes bye rays of screen. They should switch off of the screen during break and close their eyes for some time, this will relax there over-exhausted retina and prevent headaches.


11. Don't quit

Even a small step towards your success matters, every time you think about quitting takes you a step back. Know when you are about to give up and assert your will to succeed. Don't be influenced by people that have given up along the way. Your journey is unique and different. Follow your own script because everyone has a different one. Have a stable mind and take careful steps towards achieving and have fun faith in God. Work without working for the fruit of your efforts, it's in the hand of The Almighty. Success failure day-night pleasure or pain are two faces of a coin which cannot be separated. As day comes after night success will surely come after failure. Sometimes successful people also fail but it does not affect them in March because they have seen many failures in life but rather than quitting they tried to figure out the reason for their failure to correct it. So, don't quit by getting afraid of failures and pain just work hard for it and one day you will definitely be on the other side of the coin.

## 12. Don't get carried away

Have a firm straight forward courageous positive attitude for what you want. Learn to reject things which are not right for you. Don't get carried away by people's suggestions and decisions, have a firm faith in yourself and in your decisions. Saying no at the right time can save you from unpleasant situations in the future. Your personality should stand firm like Sun and no one should touch it. If you are right then stand against the crowd it, makes you unique. Don't say yes just to please, we cannot make everyone happy by compromising. Take a stand for your decision in life. Your mean in is to develop yourself so don't just go with the flow every time like a fallen leaf in a river, be like the roots which hold the tree firmly e bi making its way even through the hard ground.

13. Control your subconscious mind

Whatever we see or whatever stimulus we get we react to it from our conscious mind but it unknowingly gets saved in our subconscious mind. It stores all our emotions Desire memory feeling and conscious mind provokes them at the time of requirement. The subconscious mind feeds everything it receives whether it is good or bad important or not. Feeling our subconscious mind with anger jealousy hatred and alkynes of negativity can affect our conscious mind which can be seen in our activities. A conscious mind regulates the entry of desirable and undesirable things. If we have a powerful mind we can know what's good for us and whatnot, but weak minds get easily manipulated by all the otherworldly negativities. Our conscious mind becomes strong by giving experience having the right thoughts and having self-control. The subconscious mind can lead you to waste your time buy daydreaming, therefore your subconscious mind should not overpower your conscious mind.


14. Don't waste time

Time waits for none. It is the most precious gift given by God, and once if it is lost you can never gain it at any cost (time is priceless). Even the richest man on the earth cannot buy time. The realization of waste time creates in society of the loss done. Time management with planning and concentration is the key goal to success so note down your priorities and work on them. We all get 24 hours a day, it depends on us that how much productivity we can extract out of it. You should utilize every moment of it with planning to produce constructive output. Don't waste your time in unnecessary loitering social media gossiping sleeping daydreaming, rather use it to have some productivity.

15. Don't it bother others too much

Don't bother anybody unless their actions really do any harm to you. Keep your mind open for acceptance and try to be liberal rather than criticizing other's thoughts and feelings. Commenting judging finding faults and criticizing others shows how negative we are for the difference in the different varieties in the world. Our brains are similar but not the same people have their own opinions and thoughts regarding a point, we should learn how to respect them and try to listen to their opinions before impulsively opposing it. You can neither be perfect 9 make anyone perfect by trying to change them. A wise person who cannot be affected aura molded by other views. Become a wise person and listen to everybody but only do the things which make you feel happy.


16. Eliminate ego

Ego fills the heart with hatred and mind with anxiety and won't let you accept things or realize your mistakes. People lose relationships, job, and family just because they think their ego is more important than everything. There is a fine line between ego and self-respect which you have to understand. You should have a balance between keeping your self-respect and letting go of your ego away. don't go too low that you load yourself respect and don't go to high that you lose think because of your ego. Everything in this world is in the control of the divine power, he has created has so he can destroy us too. Therefore stay humble towards people and have faith in God, he wins show you a pathway which is away from ego and we'll lead you to a happy and successful life.

17. Stopped discrimination

do we have different in skin color have different professions belong to different cast and country speak different language and where different clothes but beneath we all have the same body. do external me look different but internal ep all have heart which have feelings in it, p all have brain which have emotion. We all eat food where clothes to hide our body inhale the same a drink the same water and use the same resources for our betterment. Mani wealth beauty our world lee object and tie knot permanent. no one is immortals everybody is this time to die someday. there is a soul in everybody which will be ultimately surrounded to god. Discrimination only creates hatred inequality E and friction in society. Try to have vision of a mother, as she doesn't disc a minute between her children we also should not disc a minute between people.

## 18. Live in the present

the happiest day of living is to live in the present and enjoy the moment. Every moment feels special if you any eliminates worries about what will happen next. Brooding about your past and wearing about your future only creates anxiety and tension. Present gives you opportunities to learn new things and build up a strong future and past gives you a lesson for not making mistakes. You cannot build a better tomorrow by regretting your past mistakes and randomly thinking about future, rather work hard today who built a letter future. Given a small moment of joy can be made memorable bye living it to the fullest.

19. Stop procrastination

Delaying work is a lazy person's job. For them tomorrow never comes and once the time is lost its lost forever. You cannot cope up with all the previous left out work at the same time; Post bonding things only keeps you lagging behind. Successful people do they work at the right time without delay. List out the things to do, and divide them by assigning the approximate time required to complete it. Keep your things in an organized manner so as to preventing wasting time in fetching them. plan your day on the previous day and wake up early in the morning to execute it because in the morning mental in a mental and physical energy is at speak, therefore start your day with finishing of the hardest and time taking task. Lagan things can only create confusion, stress and discourage at the end.

20. Love what you do; do what love

Think about what you really want to do. Come down your mind and give yourself some time alone to analyze your priorities, likes and dislikes; without your most favorable one and in which you are good at. Make plans on how to work on it and be stable and form about doing it. Don't worry about the fruits, it's not in our hand, the almighty decide it for us. put job with you don't like can only that your body and mind but not your thoughts and desires of how to get out of it. It's never too late to choose your life according to your happiness.

21. Life is the name of gift and take

Giving and taking is the law of nature. There is nothing free in this world. Anyhow we have to repay for the things we which we get in free like inherited property lotteries bribe money and free items. We are in symbiotic relationship with nature like with plants, as we give out carbon dioxide which is needed by plant as raw material to synthesize food and take oxygen given out by them. Ever since ancient times, nothing is free. when money was not invented people use to give products made by them to buy food clothes and other items of necessity. So anyhow we live in a mutual relationship of Give and take with nature, people and the almighty god.

22. Stop excessive and it and worries

Excessive worries causes anxiety and depression. Worries can be taken in a positive or negative way. Taking worries in a negative way can make you crazy and lose all your self control, while taking it in a positive way can prevent you from wasting time, doing mistakes or leading yourself to awful state. Taking things negatively in bad situations makes it more worse. We can turn every bad situation into a good one by creating a positive aura around us.

## 23. Let things go away

Nothing is permanent everything keeps on changing. Getting too much attached to something can make an emotionally weak. We have to tackle our mind that we are temporarily connected to the objects around us. Taking everything too seriously can overpower our subconscious mind over our consciousness and hamper our happiness and creates anxiety. We have to move on in every step of life and go-ahead to the next phase. Getting emotionally attached to some work or some stuffs only e create emotional trauma. Holding on your past and regretting about your failures only holds you back from being happy. Detach yourself from worldly things and focus on what you can do you with your inner conscience.

## 24. Give time to yourself

We can take care of others if we are healthy. Taking care of your mind and body is very important to try to find some time daily to pamper yourself with whatever you like. Doing exercise or yoga for or even 20 minutes a day keep your mind calm and makes your body feel fit and energetic. Treat yourself with some good food or drinks for chocolates, it releases happy hormones like and endorphins, dopamine, and serotonin. Spend some time staying away from worldly objects Technology and people and talk to yourself and evaluate your priorities likes and dislikes and your goals in life.

## 25. Thank God for what you have

A man's greediness has no limit. He wants more even though he has enough of it. But the truth is that everything belongs to God he decides how much to shower his blessings on you depending upon how truly and sincerely you work for it. Don't compare yourself with the people who have more amenities then you. Wealth property name Fame will remain here in this world but our souls have life after death. Our consequences of life after death will be based on our deeds and not on how much amenities we have. The greatest wealth is good health. Always be thankful to God for your good health and whatever you have.

## 26. It's Never too late

Never too late to start a new life to gain experience to rise from failures to make new relationships and to be happy. Hard work doesn't depend upon your age. If you really have the willpower to do something every hurdles and obstacles of life will be e invisible to you. It's the law of nature that if God closes one get for you he opens another one. You you should have the willingness to Grab the opportunities at any point in your life. As time passes you gain more experience and become strong so don't be negative towards your age because you are a better person then you were before.

## 27. Stop chronic disorganization

Chronic disorganization is a state of mental condition where air we brood too much about our pasts this organization and have fear of future disorganization. It affects our life because of the thought of disorganization message our whole day. We should have plants for your next day and make sure to complete it. We are too much associated with our environment keeping our things organized keeps our mind free from the thought of searching them. Situation disorganization means being this organized in mind and taking the wrong decision which can lead to lifetime regret or illness. chronic disorganization can be cured by keeping our mind positive before doing anything. The past which is this organized cannot be organized anymore but we can shape our future according to us. Present is the movement where you can change your life and cure chronic disorganization.

28. Have good company

We all live in a society and get affected by them. Having a good company fills you with Positive Vibes. don't compromise in choosing your friends .choose people wisely on whom you can trust. Stay away from people who speak ill about and whose thoughts don't match with yours. Breaking friendship frequently is a sign of an unstable week's mind. Stay away from people who are negative; like ok a priest cannot B between a Gang of Hooligans. Just don't go for the people who are good to you rather what's their behavior towards others too.

29. Have less expectations

Too much of Expectations hurt. Do your deeds without thinking of getting fruit. Whatever we get it is decided by God, he will provide us with fruits at the right time. Helping others is is purely a godly work which we should do you without expecting back ok anything. If the idea of getting something back comes to your mind then and the godly work just turns into your business. Even in a relationship a person cannot be perfect, mistakes happen expectations cannot be fulfilled up to the level. So expecting too much from your partner is only going to hurt you; have dual vision and try to look from here partners' side. The least expected person is the happiest person on the earth because he can adjust his mind in any circumstances.

30. We can learn from everybody in the world

Nobody's perfect but Every person is unique in their own way and we can learn a lot from them. Great people are always positive in every ups and downs of life we should learn this quality e of tolerance from them. We can learn from our mother that how she works hard to balance share life children and her family simultaneously. Even the tiniest animal-like ants and bees can give us Unity lesson like how they work ok as a team member to collect food. We should learn from our soldiers how they are risking their lives for our safety. keep your mind open to accept knowledge from experienced keep a creative Outlook on what you have learned from that person and how you can execute it in your life. We should read great stories of common people and get inspired by them to be virtuous in life.

## 31. Stop giving excuses

Giving excuses is only a way to get out of a situation but it cannot solve it ever. Only a lazy person give excuses that he doesn't have time because they want to escape from doing any sort of work. Even though they have free time I will waste it in randomly wandering loitering watching TV gossiping and reading random magazines etc. If we want to achieve something in life we have to leave back ok our lazy nature and make a schedule of everything we want to do. We all get 24 hours a day but it depends on us that how much we use it to learn something new or to be productive. It requires our soul interest to do you are thing, so, rather than giving excuses to accept your mistakes and work on them to prevent the same mistakes happening in the future.

32. Stay connected to God

Every day is like a new life, it's a gift of God; you go to bed hoping to wake up the next morning. Pray to God every night before going to bed and thank him after waking up to give you a new day filled with hope, energies and opportunities. Though you might be much in the magic of Science and Technology yet there is no power greater than the divine God. Everything in nature is controlled by him he is the mightiest and most powerful creator. He can make or destroy us based on our Karma. Whenever you feel helpless and hopeless just surrender yourself to him and pray for your well being. He will decide our destiny which will be best for us.

33. Stop overeating

There are three zones in our stomach i.e cardiac fundus and pyloric. According to science and nutrition, our cardiac part of the stomach should be empty to facilitate the churning movement of the stomach. Overeating has many e bad effects on our body, it makes a person dull and sleepy and by hampering our digestion it can cause food poisoning. It becomes difficult to breathe when your stomach is full and sometimes during sleep, the breathing process can stop due to overheating which is called sleep apnea. It can also cause heart diseases to increase our blood pressure cause cancer arthritis and type 2 diabetes. Overeating leads to obesity which lowers our self-esteem because we start feeling uncomfortable in our body D and around people who are physically fit.

34. Rapid weight loss and health habits

According to nutrition and health, rapid weight loss is not a good sign, it can cause illness, affects our mind and is of no use. You may lose some pounds by starving for days but your body craves for food so this way of losing weight cannot be e done for a longer period. Starving weakens the brain and body, lowest down our blood pressure and decreases a blood sugar level. As you know our brain needs 20% of our body's blood sugar and oxygen so during starvation inadequate amount of blood sugar is reached to brain and hampers it function. All the secretions and the metabolic processes of our body is control by the reflex of brain, so slowing down of brain slows down our metabolic activity and weekends immune system and we become more prone to diseases. "slow and steady wins the race", therefore Rapid weight loss is not a solution to become slim rather you should replace an healthy food with healthy ones and do regular exercise. As impulsive reactions does not last for long, Rapid weight loss also cannot be in the long run, as soon as you get back to your old diet after losing some pounds, your body again start gaining weight.

A good health is the greatest gift you can get from God. If we are healthy, we have the capability to win the World. We have been taught since nursery classes that we should wash your hands before and after eating to maintain personal hygiene. Many communicable diseases are spread due to lack of hygiene. 8 hour sleep is important for the proper functioning of the brain, the best time of sleeping is between 10 pm to 6 am. Regular exercise is important for a healthy brain and a fit body. Keep your health habits up to mark to lead an updated life.


35. Self medication

Self medication is a process of curing oneself with medicines without the consultation of a doctor. It is a process which is used to cure common health ailment at home. Self medication can be good for fast cure and can save the cost of consulting a doctor, but it can be dangerous because self diagnosis sometimes can go wrong, because the symptoms of some diseases are in common. Some drugs can cause allergic reaction and can lead to other diseases. Some medicines can suppress a symptom but cannot cure it which intensifies the actual disease. It does more harm than doing well so it's better to avoid self medication and consult a doctor for medication.


36. Chocolate is really helpful

Studies have shown that dark chocolate really helps to reduce stress and anxiety. On a survey of people researcher have concluded that lower level of stress hormone was released after eating 40 grams of dark chocolate every day for a week. Before and after this observation doctors duck urine and blood plasma samples of the people in the study and found that the levels of stress hormone cortisol and catecholamines where less in the sample collected after eating dark chocolates for a week. Which contains antioxidants and anti-inflammatory agents which are beneficial for brain function and cardiovascular health. It lifts up mood increases memory power immunity response to stimulus and makes our mind more active. According to research dark chocolates also lower down cholesterol levels.

37. Maintain good posture

Our body language represents our attitude towards others and towards our life. Maintaining a good posture can relieve us from many problems. If we stand walk and sit with bowed Shoulders for a prolonged period of time, our spine Benz which can cause spinal injury. Maintain a good posture even while sleeping don't sleep with your legs gold sleep on your your right arm it decreases pressure on heart and facility its function during sleep. Remaining in a good posture gives an appearance of persons confidence not only e on the outside but we are self start feeling confident from inside. There is a great relationship between mind and body, both effects each other. If your mind is happy and confident it reflects in your body language and vice versa. So by maintaining a good posture we can tackle our mind to be happy E and confident.

38. Be close to nature

We all are dependent on nature, it provides us food and fodder. Every little creature in nature has its own importance. In our daily rushing life we are too much far away from nature and close to all harmful things like noise pollution air pollution land pollution and water pollution. All this affects us in an adverse way. Take out some time from your busy busy schedule to go near nature to calm down your soul. You can go to some park forest riverside lakes or even Gardens. The soothing scenery of nature fills our mind with joy calmness and releases our stress and anxiety. Nature gives a small than what it takes from us. As life is the name of Give and take we should not only take advantage of nature but should also do something for it. We should keep our natural environment clean stop deforestation and plant more trees. The most important thing to be alive is Oxygen food and water in all this comes from nature so we have to take care of it for us to be alive.

39. Weather condition also affects us

Heat cold rain noise pollution everything affects our health. We are seriously heading towards extreme global warming every year. Due to it, we experience extreme heat extreme cold and extreme rainfall at some places resulting in floods. Although we are endothermic homeotherms outer extreme environment affects our. Enzymes function in a specific range of temperature if our body temperature rises or falls down from that range our metabolic functions are hampered. Exposure to extreme heat for a prolonged period can cause heat strokes extreme thirst diarrhea low blood pressure headache dizziness vomiting and painting. In extreme cold conditions, our body fails to maintain its temperature and our metabolism cases, it can cause frostbite, hypothermia and even death. In general 40-80 decibels is a normal range of hearing, generally sound above 85 decimal is harmful for us and prolonged exposure of it can cause hearing impairment. All type of pollutions adversely affects us. We should not only avoid all the extremists but try to cure them by taking care of air off of Mother Earth.

40. Colors affect your personality

Every color is made up of different frequency and wavelength which has different vibrational effects in our mind. Choose the right color which suits best to your personality. Everybody has different favorite colors which shows that their brains are differently active. Every color represents different meaning like- Violet-spirituality and elegance and royalty Indigo- self-awareness reduce irritability  Blue- calmness hope truth and lowers the body temperature and increases the consciousnesses Green- it is a cool color and gives positive effect improve vision resembles growth balance health wealth and fertility Yellow- give positive Vibes and is a stress buster live religious aura positivity clean mind and firmness. Orange- helps in curing diseases like customer kidney ailments represents creativity and ambition. Red- represents passion enthusiasm love excitement power anger and danger.

As mentioned above that every color has a different impact on us choose your home an office ambiance. Every color is unique but it's not necessary that it combines with every color. Wrong combination of colors can create a bad impact to the viewers. So choose your colors wisely to create a positive Vibes around you. Where softly e colored dresses, it reflects your calm and stable personality.

## 41. Keep nature clean

Not only keeping your home should make you happy, clean your environment too. you can't clean the whole city on your own but you can do your part by keeping your society clean. Every day turns and turns off waste is produced and it is the most alarming situation. Damping-off of garbage in rivers and oceans pollutes it and harms marine life. Every kind of pollution unknowingly somehow affects us. A heap of garbage causes pollution gives out bad smell and it is home for many germs and parasites which affects our health. A clean environment gives an impression of well-behaved citizens living there. Don't spread litter wherever you go. Our mother earth provides us life so we should take care of air off her by serving her.

# 42. Everything has its advantage and disadvantage

All the worldly objects are like a coin which has two faces one good and the other one bad. If a person is negative according to you he might be positive in the views of someone else, it's just a way of seeing a person from one side of the coin. Things which has advantage Shirley do have some disadvantage. Every aspect has its opposite which can be separated from it. A thing which gives you pleasure might give you pain sometimes. With great happiness comes great responsibility, like if you get promoted in a job you will get more money e respect indignity but you will have the pressure to handle everybody is work and have to work ok or more things then you did before. Even if every situation has its pros and cons, we need to learn to enjoy the process of the situation. If a situation comes when you find it as a disadvantage don't forget to flip the coin and see the other side of it. Before judging a person and drawing and conclusion about him try to you look at him from both sides of the coin. And before taking any decisions you should think about its pros and cons, it will lead you to a better decision. Don't get much affected by the dual nature of the world, neither get elated in success nor grieve in failure.

## 43. Don't lie, be honest

truth prevails in the long run no matter how much we try to hide it. A lie can save you from a situation for some time but it does not prevail for a longer period. As you start line one thing leads to another and you start flying more to cover up your previous lie. Work is link praising to God, we can like to everybody even to ourselves but we cannot lie to God, so be honest and dedicated towards your work as our praising. Karma will always Revolt us for honesty and will punish for cheating. We should do everything with honesty without being double-faced, our thoughts should match our deeds. If we don't like ok a work we should not do it or if we don't like a person we should remain away from them rather than being friends and then speaking ill about name to others. Be honest in saying whatever you don't like lying is there in the situation can put you in adverse conditions.

## 44. Change yourself before changing others

Don't think yourself better than others Raja think OK then better than you and try to improve yourself. Looking down on people and commenting on how they should leave what do they do and what should they do to improve themselves you should look down on yourself try to find your false and weakness. Each person's contribution to changing the world matters a lot. Trying to change others will not help you if you don't change others. Ki positive thinking Good gesture and cleanliness around you and let people learn from you. Like ok, a teacher can not spread his knowledge unless he himself learn it. A mother with great values makes her child visor by sharing her virtues. In a medical school, only a doctor can make a doctor hi spirits his wisdom to his students. Likewise, if you don't change yourself you cannot make a change in others. Your wife's of goodness will spread among others and they will start changing themselves buy induction.

45. Freeing yourself from mindless guilt

Mindless guilt can lead to depression and trauma. Convince your mind that you have tried your best but things happen according to fate. Don't judge yourself to be a bad person. Stop blaming yourself for everything which doesn't feels right to you. If we don't get out of it, we will be blaming ourselves for the rest of our life. Forgive yourself and accept your mistakes because no one is perfect and mistakes happens, so don't punish yourself for the wrong done. Things which are meant to occur will happen.

## 46. Overcome your fears

Fear is a state of mind. It means we are negative about a thing. Every person has a fear of different things. Like if a person is curd from a dog but some other person does not so there might is something which makes that person not to hear about the dogs. So he should try to see the dog from that person's view and evaluate his fears. If we let fear death overpower it takes over mind and body d and charges a bus with anxiety. According to the law of attraction what we fear the most will chase us more. If you think of getting a disease we start to show symptoms of it. Fears are just challenges in our life so rather running away from, it intentionally faces it, and if we are strong enough to fight, we can go through them and come out as a strong bold and firm person.

47. Never stop learning

The world is changing every minute. Every minute something new is happening. Every day some new inventions are being made. Every are new news comes up which gives us a lesson. We should learn from other people mishap to be safe. God gives us the opportunity to learn from everything we just have to keep a vision and will Power of Learning. Even a small kid with a pure heart can teach you lessons of life. Don't think yourself superior if you have much knowledge, because no one can have perfect knowledge there is always a chance to learn something new till our last breath. Don't think yourself as self-sufficient everybody is unique but no one is perfect and there is no age restriction in learning. Learn from your elders who have more experience in the field of life. Our brain is always rewire itself and become sharp whenever we learn something new. Gaining a little knowledge from every field will do no harm to you but it will make you smart and intelligent in front of others.

48. Put your thoughts into words

Writing down everything that comes in your mind keeps it as a hard copy E and won't let it vanish from your mind because you can recall it whenever you want. Writing down your thoughts helps you to execute them properly like a writer writes down whatever comes in his mind and create great stories and motivations. Don't feel your mind with lots of Thoughts let it out in a piece of paper and make space in your brain for new thoughts. Our brain delete pieces of information and thoughts which are not important for us by the process of apoptosis. Therefore to remember the things note down so that you can have a clear vision of what came into your mind.

## 49. No work is big or small

There is a ladder to every achievement which you have to climb up to gain success. The landers starts with the first small step without taking that step we cannot build a strong future. To build a strong future v we have to make our base stronger it may collapse anytime. You cannot skip the little bits of word and think of doing something big this is a false success. No work is big or small it's just a matter of choice or preference. It all depends on our thinking that are we really dedicated to making a strong base for our future and are we really willing to climb up the first step towards Our success. It depends on us that how do we execute that work. With our attitude and willingness to work we can take any small work to higher-level or can bring down big works to a smaller level.

50. Be more productive

In today's world of rush and competition if we don't be more productive in less time we will be left back in the race of the world. You should work hard with the right strategies to beat everybody in this race. Productivity in any work or study comes from planning concentration execution and honesty. If we plan our work we will have a clear vision of what things we have to do and by concentrating on it we can stop wasting time. Execution of work with the right and updated strategies is important, doing things haphazardly is only a waste of resource time and energy. Be honest about your work don't leave it in the middle. Being productive is more important than working for hours and hours. Because the work hard work remain confined to us but the productivity e is seen by the whole world.

51. Control your fluctuating mind

A fluctuating mind cannot achieve anything because it jumps from one thing to another and never remain stable until results. There are a lot of options in everything to choose from and often we get confused between them. A fluctuating minded person sometimes we end up choosing the wrong option and regretting later, but if the same case happens with a strong-minded person hi rather than regretting the wrong choice tries to find out what advantage it could give to him. A fluctuating mind always in some thinking what it would have been if it shows the other option. Control your fluctuating mind and keep a firm faith in your decision even though it sometimes leads you to grief.


52. Don't blame others

We are in full control of our conscious mind. Strong-minded person nose what's good and what's bad for him. Our subconscious mind feels in all the negativity we get from outside and if our subconscious mind is overpowering our conscious mind we may do mistakes and later on when we realize about it we blame others. So don't get any negativity fill in your mind. Keep your conscious mind power and take responsibility for whatever decision you take in life. Blaming things on others is just a sign of week mind which cannot take responsibility e of any bad happened. That kind of Mind cannot achieve anything in life because it runs away from the adversity never wants to face them. As you know no that you can overcome your fears and failure only by facing them. A conscious person and take responsibility for his decisions; even though it's good or bad, he never blame it on someone else.

53. Staying in bad situations with more calm and awareness

Tragedies and misfortunes are a part of everybody is life. Whether you like them or not it will come across some part of your life and you have to overcome through it by keeping calm and having faith in God. A strong-minded person cannot get much affected by this misfortunes. The sooner you learn to accept and then reconcile with the impending calamity, the sooner you will be at peace with yourself. You should learn to adjust to the impending disaster as quickly as possible and start acting again at the same speed.

Some people make out a catastrophe of their situation. They tend to overreact in every situation and lose their calm. They make their mind dull and negative in adverse conditions. People with this kind of attitude tend to feel easily. Remain depressed and feel helpless for a long time and remain in this miserable condition until they get out of that emotional impact. We don't realize how much time and energy they have best stay in just regretting in there misfortune. Treasuries and which sport shoes are a part of life we cannot ignore them but we have to face them strongly. Instead of getting shocked by them Kam and think a way to get out of it.

## 54. Keep a smile on your face

The first thing a person sees in others is his face. Our face is our first impression. By our facial gesture, one can analyze what's going on in your head. Our gestures and emotions are interrelated to each other. You can't have a natural smile when you are sad. You can't laugh naturally when you are angry. Our mood is reflected in gestures and gestures can change our mood. So take advantage of your gesture to lighten up your mood. Always keep a natural smile on your face which will reflect your true attitude towards life. The easiest way to get involved with them is to make people feel comfortable and have a smile on your face. It sends out positive vibes around you.

## 55. Enjoy every little thing

If you have a positive attitude or being happy e even a piece of chocolate can make you happy. Always be thankful to the giver. Don't wait for big things to happen to be happy. You can enjoy every moment of the day. Happiness is a state of mind it does not reside in objects. Happiness can't be purchased it can only be experienced. People with a negative attitude on everything never remain happy even if they are provided with all the accommodations they want. A person who wants to be happy will find his happiness in small Perks of life no matter how small it is.

## 56. Don't have fear of death

No one is immortal. Death is a natural phenomenon. If you are born you have to die someday. It is a face from which you can't back off. If you have fear of anything else you can avoid it but you can't avoid death. Death is a boundary between physical life and Astral life. In life after death, we will not have a physical body but our soul will remain. This physical world is only a phase between two Astral life Where God send us to self evaluate and do good deeds to make our Astral life happy. It's a cycle of physical and afterlife where you do these in physical life and they are evaluated by God in our Astral life. So without wearing death lead a happy life by helping others and spreading happiness. By evaluating our d in previous life god writes our destiny for the next life.

## 57. Don't take revenge

Don't bring your mental energy in thinking about Revenge of something in done to you. God is there watching everything all the goods and all the bands. He is the one who will punish the evil ones. A person has to suffer the consequences of his bad deeds in this world itself. Learn to forgive. When you forgive a person whether he deserves forgiveness or not your heart feels like in your mind feels stress-free from the thought of Revenge. The burden of Revenge creates hatred anxiety in your soul it harms you more than that person. Just forgive and watch Karma do its job.

## 58. Don't be doubtful

Doubting everyone is a sign of negative mentality. Doubting your partner can create a barrier between your relationship. Have faith in people you love. If a person cheats you he cheats his conscience first, forgive them and let them suffer from the law of Karma. If you doubt everybody you cannot work with them because the world is based on hope up and trust. Trust is the building block of a relationship every relation is based on trust. Doubt fills our mind with suspicion tension anxiety and hatred towards others. If it becomes difficult for you to deal with people around you, just surrender your hope and expectations to God and have full faith in him whatever he decides is always right for us.

## 59. Build more confidence

Self confidence can be built if you think you can do it. Don't doubt yourself and don't be a victim of the bad situation. Never think yourself less than anyone else, if they can do it you can also do it. Self confidence helps us to overcome our fears. We should command ourselves to take a step ahead to fight from our fears. Come out of your comfort zone to set your limits high to gain more confidence and expose yourself to the fears you have.

60. Laugh everyday

Working whole day long can make you dull and lifeless. Add laughter to your boring day by reading some jokes means watching some comedy videos. You can even chat with your friends laugh and cherish your old memories with them. A little sarcasm to your words. Don't be too serious to make yourself look intelligent and serious. Sometimes being stupid is also good. Everything would be in balance your intelligence your stupidity. Even bad memories with friends become stupid if we look back and we laugh at them. When we laugh endorphins are produced in an increased amount in our body which acts as a natural painkiller. Laughter relieves from stress anxiety worries depression and sadness and nervousness. Even while speaking in public start with the humor it will make the environment light and I will reduce your nervousness and you will feel free to speak everything without the fear of being judged

61. Don't try to know your future try to make your future

No one knows their destiny. No future teller can tell our future. No astrology will work if you decide to make your future. Being anxious about what will happen tomorrow can do no good to you rather it will fill your mind with nervousness. To build a better tomorrow you have to work on it today. You are capable to take your destiny on your own hands. Don't waste your time in subconsciously thinking about your future. Bring your thoughts into action to change your destiny. You can build up your future by being firm at your goals and taking progressive steps towards it.

## 62. Don't run behind money

Some people only want to earn more and more money even though it is of no use to them. Their mind only runs behind to earn money either way. They don't give time to their family and at the end they are only left with money and not memories. More money and property needs more handling. It creates anxiety and fear of losing. The person always remains busy in earning money and rather than spending it for its happiness. Do the money can give you all the luxury to your life it will create more tension. Try to have a moderate balance between earning and spending. Use your money for your happiness. Go on vacation with your family. You cannot take the money to Your Grave. It's a worldly object and will remain here. Money might come and go but your memories and happiness will remain till your last breath.

63. Control your anger

Anger is a sign of weakness. A weak mind which can't convince a person with the power of his words tries to express it in the form of anger.Wise people always remain calm and stable in every situation. So they don't need to express their disappointment in anger. Your angry behavior makes a bad personality in your surrounding. Anger send negative Vibes around you and people will remain to talk to you and you will prefer to stay away from you. Any work can be done without showing anger.

## 64. Learn to tolerate

Don't let hate, bad comments miss behavior enter into your subconscious mind. It gets stored there. Keep your subconscious mind strong. Don't let anything bother you much. The people do whatever they want to if it does not what do harm to you then tolerate it. Even if something bad is done to you just forgive and let it go. Keeping misdoings in mind only pressurize our minds. A tolerant person can cross all the hurdles of his pathway to achieve his goal. A strong-minded person can tolerate things easily. Tolerating is not worthy when something is doing harm to you and mankind. You should raise your voice against it. Raise your voice in the right way and not by just shouting showing anger going on Rallye Acura. Find out solutions which can really work.

65. World can run without a person

Nothing is permanent we all are temporary worldly objects. Nothing can be present everywhere every time except air. Don't take pride in your existence. The world can run without us. We are here to 2-hour job and not to run this planet. Our creator is our destructor. Everything is in his hands. Mass and energy of this planet is fixed neither our but didn't increase the mass of earth not our death will decrease it. We are here to do our part of work under the Guardians Of The Almighty. Don't be sad if your loved ones pass out. Death is not in our control. Birth and death are in the hands of The Almighty.

## 66. Don't fight over religion

All people are born the same we have same blood same body we all eat food we all sleep we all work for a living we all have feelings we all have faith in God and we all will die one day. Every religion teaches to be honest faithful loving caring strong exacta. Don't compare your religion with others. They are just a path to reach god. There is only one God who is superior of all. Respect each God do you don't believe in them. Don't try to put your believes in others' mind. Our destiny is the same that is death. We don't know what's life after death. So we should do good deeds in the pathway of God rather than making conflict between religion.

67. Don't keep your mind idle

an idle mind is overpowered by subconscious mind and it gets filled with all kinds of negativity so always try to keep your mind busy and have some goals to accomplish we all are here on earth to achieve something so don't live aimlessly life is very precious our purpose in life is not only to to die but to do something to achieve happiness have some short term and long term goals a non-directional mind only harms the world if we are getting benefit from the world we should also surf for it life is not for wasting time in useless and aimless pursuits.

## 68. Solve one problem at a time

We always have more than one problem in life but if we try to solve them all simultaneously our mind gets confused and we cannot solve even one problem try to get out from a single problem at a time by giving your Full focus on how to solve it if you solve a problem at a time and come out of it you will feel encouraged to solve another one but if you  try to solve all at a time you are mental energies and concentration level gets divided into each problem and you will get no output.

## 69. Keep your surrounding beautiful

Install good photos in your wallpaper. Use light color bed sheets it gives a cooling effect to the eye. Have a beautiful painting on your wall. Keep your things organized it gives a soothing effect. Hang a picture of your loved ones. Keep things that make you feel positive and powered. Pictures create positive and negative Vibes so you can put up the picture of the person you idolize it can fill you with confidence power whenever you see it. Install a picture of your goal it will everyday make you remind of your goal and to Quill in any circumstances. Science has proved that whatever a pregnant woman sees affects her child. So to make your child a positive person, install good moral pictures.

## 70. Have self-control

Having a balance of emotion and action is very important in every situation. We should neither overreact response in a dull manner. Self-control means having a lot of patience, strictness and not getting carried away in the moment. Controlling ourselves can prevent us from doing mistakes. Too much of vulnerability is a sign of weakness and dependence; Keeping our emotions within us makes our mind strong. Mind can also take up a lot of negative advice, comments and become easily stressed. Keep your personality and your brain strong by having control over yourself.

## 71. Don't waste your energy unnecessarily

Some people try to satisfy others too much but in the long run that they had done mod for others than for himself. People don't appreciate once you stop teasing them so all you're your efforts go into vain. our mental energy can also be drain by thinking ill about others. Here we are not talking about losing your metabolic energy because by giving out the extra metabolic energy stored in your body you feel active. All our mental energies lie in our thinking. Our thoughts create an aura around us whether it is positive or negative. It is important to drain away all our negative thoughts and fill our mind with positive desires.

72. Be Independent and take your own decisions

Some of US have the habit of asking others to decide for themselves. This indicates that we have a weak mind lacking self-confidence. We must always try to solve our are problems within ourselves without consulting it with others. Sometimes we should consult with others but the final solution to our problem should be taken by ourselves. People who depend upon others for running their lights Are Never successful. The reason behind many e successful people is that they have taken risks and independent decisions in their life.

73. Learn to appreciate

We must learn to appreciate others for their good deeds. This helps in increasing them and creates a healthy and happy atmosphere around us. Seeing good things in others will always help us to stay mentally positive and cheerful. No matter how bad a person is but there is always a good side of his. We should also appreciate God for or whatever he has given to us. Be thankful for the gift of life irrespective of who you give deference to. Take a few minutes of your time after waking up and give thanks. Remember that we are all children of God. Every person on this planet is a child of God. Given our children are God's children because they are directly answerable to him and not through us. He is our Final Destination. We all are sent by God on this planet to serve some purpose which we should carry out sincerely because one day after death we have to answer him.


74. Don't misunderstand others

Some people have the habit of misunderstanding others. They always feel that others are intending to insult or hurt them by their comments. They take up every conversation as an equipment to fight or to debate. Messenger standings always create problems in a relationship, it is the main cause of breaking off of many relationships. Misunderstanding can stress out our mind and does affect our thoughts.

The problem of misunderstandings develops because of the feeling of separation from others. So to avoid this problem one should have trust in their beloveds.

## 75. Think less and do more

Some people waste a lot of their time bye buy indulging in their thoughts. Some of the US also create a scenario in our mind and think about it continuously which is happening in there real life. This wastes our time very much and distract us from doing our work. People also think about their goals too much rather than working on it. This makes them lack behind in their work. So we should always have a balance between our thoughts and work. We should avoid unnecessary thoughts and ID try I too to work ok more and more so as to be e happy E and successful.

76. Learn to be happy alone

As you know nothing is permanent in this world, everything every person and every situation come in our life for a certain period of time and there for a reason. We are born alone and will die alone. Though we remain close to our friends and family but everyone has their own life and duties. No one can be always available for you so when you feel alone don't make sad and think that you are not important to them. As we grow up we have more responsibilities then spending time with our loved ones. Do it is important to give time to your friends and family but it is also important to give time to yourself. People may leave and Expectations may hurt, so learn to be happy alone.

77. Don't complain about everything

Some people complain about everything even though it's fine. The always carry negative mentality towards everything in the world. Their mind is full of Criticism and they always feel that they are only the righteous person. Their mind always filled with tension of everything falling out of there way. Learn to appreciate everything even if it is small or big. Complaining about everything is a way of overreacting in all circumstances. There is nothing wrong with complaining about things which harms you or the society and nature. But having a thought that everything will harm you will attract negative wife towards you which really start showing symptoms of affecting your mind feeling it with stress and anxiety and interferes with your life.

78. Don't ill-treat a person

A person who is in any kind of relationship with you like- a boss and employee, a husband and wife, brother and sister,  father and son or even friend, expect something from you. Save wish to have a good relationship in which you both respect each other. Treating a person can let your dignity down in the eyes of that person. In any kind of relationship another person is not a slave, he desires to have some honor for his existence. God help center with a unique quality to live our life and Excel in things in which we are good at. A person can have tolerance power but there is a limit to everything, if you keep different respecting a person he will feel that you have lowered down his dignity so much that nothing is left with him to protect, so he will start a revolt against you.

79. Don't get addicted to social media

Though media and social media sound the same but are different. Through media, u can have information from all over the world of the people and calamities that are highlighted. Media remain confined to some aspects and boundaries, but social media has no boundaries. It is an open platform of creativity; as creativity has no end, social media never ceases to entertain us. It is a very vast platform than media where common people from all around the world can get connected. Not only it connects the people but also spreads creativity, motivation, helps in spreading business and lot more. There are many uses of social platform which we can extract out by using our capabilities.

In recent times social media addiction has become the most common addiction all over the world.as people are getting connected to each other through mobile phones, they are indulging more in false connection with strangers. Unnecessarily chatting and watching videos wastes our time and makes us addicted to it because it's a never-ending platform. It always keeps us busy in watching different things which are of no use to us.

80. Don't spread hatred

Spreading hatred is the most ill deed you can do. Not only you should not spread hatred but also you should stop others from doing it. There are many ways through which hatred can be spread like through public speaking, through media or social media, through forward messages etc. Hatred can even be spread at home; therefore watch your words before u speak ill at home. This world can only run happily only if you spread love. Hatred can only cause war and deaths.

## 81. Everything happens for a reason

There is a reason for everything nothing happens by any chance for accident. Everything in the universe is bound by a relationship of cause and effect. Whatever circumstances you are facing now you have done some work in the past to come to this moment. Your deeds from the past still have an effect on present, unless it's completely evaluated, you cannot have a new cause in life, unless our fast causes are resolved completely we cannot be happy forever. So we have to change our mental attitude in confronting the incidents and problems that happened in our past. Don't view your past cause this as a burden, consider them as a project and as a mean that will help you to grow stronger.

These are not the incidents which are to be focused upon, it is based on our mental attitude that how we respond to the past causes. As the world is a dual nature it is neither good nor bad, Everything depends upon how we will look at it.

82. Don't let Technology make you lazy

Technology has been developed for our betterment. Vehicles are made to connect the world for traveling and for shipments of goods. Equipment is made to make people's life comfortable and media is for connecting people all over the world. Technology is very useful till we use it in limits. Excessive use of Technology can lead to its misuse and make us lazy.

Following are some tips to minimize the use of Technology to prevent us from being lazy and becoming more active-

- Don't use a vehicle if you are going to nearby. Walking for that small distance will keep your body free from fatigue.
- If you have to go away don't take a cab from the front of your house. Walk for some distance and then use a vehicle for transportation.
- Always don't use washing machine for washing clothes. Wash some of your clothes by your hand.
- Don't play all the indoor games in the mobile phone. Have some real-life games.
- Reduce online shopping. Go out with your family and friends to shop, it allows you to spend time

with your friends and family and it gives happiness.

- Don't search for everything in mobile regarding your studies. Visit the library, read books, make notes in pen and paper.
- Keeping notes in the form of a photo in your mobile and reading from it can affect your eyesight.
- Prevent using air conditioner for or a long time. Sitting in an air-conditioned room all day long can make you lazy and adjustable in the outer environment.
- Shut down your phone and go out to play.
- Don't just chat with your friends on a mobile phone, go out and meet them.

## 83. Don't misuse Technology

Excessive use of Technology can lead to its misuse. If it is used in a wrong way it can affect nature and animals. Radiations caused by networking Towers are the reason for the death of many birds.  Misuse of Technology can also be done in other ways like spreading hate initiating war killing others. as you know everything has its advantages and disadvantages Technology also has a lot of advantages and can have devastating disadvantages. Today's technology is so forward that we can reach to the moon and even destroy the earth within seconds. The most dangerous creation of Technology is hydrogen bomb which can destroy the whole world with the blink of an eye. It depends on us that are we extracting advantages from technology or we doing harm to us by misusing it. So Use technology whenever you needed but don't take it to a level which can harm the nature and your mind.

## 84. Don't backbite

Backbiting is considered as a sin. Never backbite behind anyone and stay away from people who speak is about other people because with this kind of nature they become friends with everybody take their secrets and speak ill about it to others. Karma takes Revenge for every sin done. If you do harm to others by speaking ill about them to others, you will have to face the Revenge of Karma.

## 85. Don't create a communication gap

Differences between two people can only be decreased by having a conversation. Fighting in any circumstances only makes the situation was but having a scam conversation problem can be sorted out. Communication between parents and that children is very important to understand what's going on in their life. Whenever fight with your partner don't just sit there being angry but sit calmly with your partner and talk to them. Communication gap only create distance and problems between relationships. My talking to each other you can understand the other people's point of view and resolve your conflict

## 86. You can't be master of all things

Don't think of expertise in all feels we are not meant to be perfect but to be unique. You cannot be fully independent of others you cannot grove your own food make your own clothes and shoes with your own house makes your own atmosphere. Therefore we live in a society in which different people do different work for living and somehow we all are dependent on each other. Keeping knowledge of everything is good but trying to do everything is not worthy. You will lose time in doing all the things and you cannot excel in a particular job. Do our mind can store and all amount of knowledge yet all the data need to be record every once in a while to keep it fixed. Try to explain in one field in which you are really interested in this way your mind is concentrated in one job and it does not forget stuff about it.

87. Learn to adjust

Everything in life doesn't go in our way. Only liberal and positive mind can adjust everywhere. World is very complex and people have different opinions on certain things. We should try to understand and respect every once views rather than criticizing them. We cannot run the world according to our house; as newton's third law safe every action has an equal and opposite reaction so there y are certain forces that act against us. if we fight with the opposing forces we gonna revert back but if we want to move forward we have to learn to adjust with the opposition forces to forward equally bit it.

88. Don't be selfish

The lost the nature is to give and take. Whatever we want we have to give something for it. Natures lost the more you give the more you get so don't be selfish. Great your happiness don't keep can find it to yourself. God shower his blessings on people who self lately help others. If you don't share your things don't expect to get anything from others. If you don't hear your love you will not be loved by anyone else. As the Mother Nature selflessly provide amenities to us we should also serve. Milan selfish people always have hatred and malice in their heart. Don't become selfish schedule joy and positive wife to others.

## 89. Have good manners

Education reflex in our manners. In our sizzler's life good manners mattress a lot it reflects our value and personality. Whenever you meet someone great them by saying hi and asking how are you. You should use the words like thank you please sorry whenever needed this shows year generosity towards others. We learn good manners from our elders so don't be in full it went towards children because they learn from us. Our manners can also be moved by our company so choose a good company which teachers you to behave well. Licking somebody's secret and gossiping about others are bad manners. The main away from the people who speak inappropriately. Your good manners can make your place in other hearts.

90. Don't waste anything

Wasting is a result of buying in excess. In order to curb this, you need to have the understanding that consumption and disposal goes hand in hand. Cutting consumption is not all that we can do in a bid to avoid wastage. We can still adopt mechanisms that will see to it that we remain waste less. Normally less consumption would not be praised by the media in mainstream this is because every industry is trying to make profit. In order to adopt tastelessness, one needs to understand that the waste has a tolling effect to the environment.

91. Enjoy the word not the fruit

It is truly said that the fruit of our own hard work is the sweetest. We must learn to get satisfied by our work and not by the consequences. As the consequences are not in our hands so we should never depend our happiness on it. The fruits of our work is only in the hands of God. We always have a thought in our mind that we don't get what we deserve but that's absolutely wrong. God always gives us what we deserve but only at the right time. So we should always enjoy our work without thinking about the fruits of it. So why to get mad about whatever will be the results? Just enjoy each and every part of your work and let the result be in the hands of our almighty.

92. Don't try to change others

If we look closely in ourselves we will get to know that most of our time and energy we waste in trying to change others. We never think that sometimes we also so need to be changed. We always think that others are the reason behind our sorrow and unhappiness in our life and unless they won't change their self we won't be happy. The true fact is that we can't change any person by convincing them nor by forcefully. Everyone has their own way of thinking.so we should try to adjust with everyone and in every circumstance without thinking of changing anybody's thoughts and behavior. However if you apply force in changing somebody, their ego becomes more adamant and they will never agree to change themselves is the characteristic of ego to not to say yes or I agree.so we should try to remain happy with whatever kind of person we are dealing with in our life and learn to accept everybody s flows and try to adjust with them.

93. Reduce collection of worldly things

Normally we assume that we collect equipment and gadgets more than any of our needs. We humans have a habit of comparing our lives and ourselves with others. We are never satisfied with whatever we have. we always want more and more in our lives. this creates a feeling of jealousy and hatred towards others. we always want our stuffs like our electronic gadgets our houses etc better than others. It also creates a competition between us. By seeing others thing we get a feeling of buying unnecessary things which are in not use of us. This can also trouble us in some way or the other. We should always try to stay happy with our own stuffs without comparing our lives with others. Our happiness should be within our family and not by the attractive and expensive things. these gadgets not only harm ourselves but also the environment. So by keeping a little distance from these things and having everything in an appropriate amount can make us healthy and happy forever.

94. Eat better and health

Having healthy food is very necessary to keep our body in proper shape and to live a healthy lifestyle. Nutrition is a very important part of leading a healthy lifestyle. A nutritional diet along with physical activity helps us to stay away from many chronic diseases and promote overall of our health. Eating healthy food is not compulsory but it is referred to as healthy eating is what will eventually determine the lifespan of an individual. A balanced diet contains all the nutrients in an appropriate manner. We need all types of Nutrition for our body two function properly. Additional, the type of lifestyle we have directly e determines our health. Eating healthy food rather than eating junk food that is available in the market can reduce the risk of many types of diseases like obesity, diabetes and other heart-related diseases. Eating healthy food can also reduce the risk of cancer.

95. Reduce velocity of mind

In most of the people's mind thoughts Run one after another in a tremendous velocity. Their mind is not still for even a moment. There is always something running on their mind like planning working moving and tensing. Gradually it becomes a Habit for them and their mindsets in this velocity. Even when there is nothing to worry about this kind of people keep on searching for opportunities to get worried. When they have nothing to do they only think about getting some work instead of relaxing their mind at that moment.

Slowing down your minds can slow down the number of thoughts running in it. A high-velocity mind can never keep calm and sometimes reacts anxiously and shows anger. Velocity of Mind generally remains high during negative emotion and stress. A high-velocity mind having an enormous amount of thoughts is a sign of a weak and uncontrolled mind. A controlled mind keeps certain thoughts within it which are important in the present moment and only focuses on them. Slow down your mind by taking only present activities in your hand. Don't remain in the memory of the past and don't think about the future. When you think too much about past and future it leads to poor performance of the present task in hand.

# 96. Always remain optimistic

Always remain optimistic even if you fail in doing a task. There is no force on earth and in heaven which can stop you from achieving success. You only require a determined mine with firm faith in God. Not even a slightest effort made by you will never go in vain. The law of nature is if you suffer from discomfort and illness now you will surely get fruits later or sooner. So don't quit even if things don't fall in your way. There is no need to be upset when you fail as success and failure are two sides of a coin which are inseparable. If you feel today surely you will be successful tomorrow.

# 97. Do regular exercise

Exercising everyday fills you with motivation that you can do anything. Different types of exercises like stretching aerobics and cardio releases tension Titans up your muscles and thus leads to muscular relaxation. As our body and mind power are connected so relaxation of muscles leads to relaxation of our mind. Daily exercises strengthen our lungs heart and increase our stamina and power of resistance. It keeps us fit positive and away from diseases. Show me a daily routine of doing physical exercise

## 98. Remain above diseases

Our body is a physical machine and it is subjected to all kinds of trauma like pain and diseases. the problems come to our body depending upon how much we take care of it. Although we take care of body d by physical means but the most important thing is mental health. Our mind controls our body so if we are mentally sick everything attacks our body. If we remain negative about being healthy any diseases can attack us. So take care air of both mental and physical health.

## 99. Dispose of rubbish regularly

Old rubbish gets collected in our home and workplace for overlay time if we don't clean them. Keeping all those old things required maintenance and we waste our energy and time in doing that. We should dispose of our old waste materials to give space to new things. Disposing does not me throwing away your old items. There are many needy people in this world, donate your old things to them.

## 100. Don't feel lonely and bored

A lonely person can't face himself and runs behind objects and other people in this world to keep his mind occupied. When he does not have all this to keep him engaged he feels bored. He does not realizes that a person can be happy alone. As happiness is a state of mind and it does not reside in worldly objects, we should learn to be happy even though we don't have things to keep us busy or people to keep us engaged.

## 101 (gift ☺). More success

Success comes in determination for achieving goal. More creative person are capable of having more success. Don't stop gaining knowledge in every aspect of life, it helps you to move forward with the generation and keep your thoughts and strategies updated. Stay away from distraction; don't let anyone stagnate your thought. Time management also plays a very important role in achieving success. Without managing your time you cannot get more results and in more in less time.

# Conclusion

By practicing all the above affirmations daily, you will find that gradually your mind is being cleansed and your aura is becoming free of all impurities. I hope you become unbiased, strong, pure, positive and free from all fears. By gaining knowledge on all topics mentioned you will learn how to tackle your mind to balance it between stress and happiness. Don't lodge subconscious mind with any negativity.

Practice all the exercises and good habits to maintain your physical and mental health. After reading this book you should have complete control on your thoughts and desire for filling it with all the positive assertions. Make your personality strong that no evil can contaminate you. Keep laughing every day and spread love and joy to all your loved ones. Be stable and calm so that you don't linger between the extremes. Fill your heart with joy and not with grief of sorrow and misery. Always be close to God, he is the controller of our life. Do good deeds because sooner or later the day will come when we have to answer him about our actions.

I hope that my readers enjoyed this book. I wish you always remember all the tips I suggested for being happy and positive throughout your life. Recall all the positive affirmations regularly and practice all the exercises every day to maintain good health.